6 80
pets
8112

Physical Characteristics of the Clumber Spaniel

(from the American Kennel Club breed standard)

Back: Straight, firm, long and level.

Tail: Well feathered and set on just below the line of back.

Hindquarters: The thighs are heavily muscled. The stifle shows good functional angulation, and hock to heel is short and perpendicular to the ground.

Coat: The body coat is dense, straight and flat.

Color and Markings: The Clumber is primarily a white dog with lemon color or orange color markings. The body should have as few markings as possible.

Rear feet: Not as large or as round as on the front feet but compact, with thick pads and are of substantial size.

D1265518

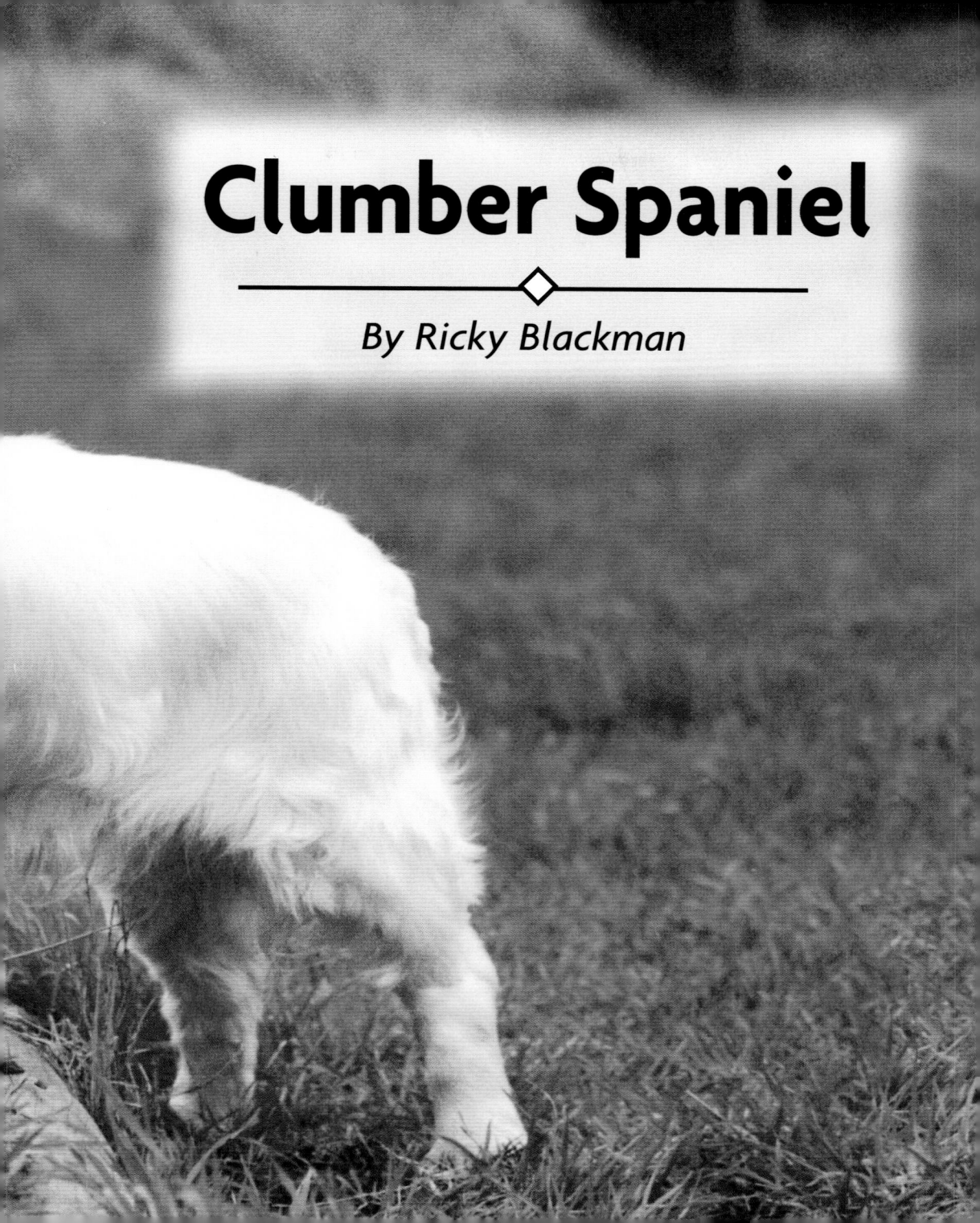

Clumber Spaniel

By Ricky Blackman

Contents

8 History of the Clumber Spaniel

Examine the various theories about the origins of the Clumber Spaniel. Whether English, French or Spanish, the breed has developed into a unique and recognizable gundog around the world. Although its popularity has never been comparable to that of the other spaniels, the charming and talented Clumber remains one of the dog world's best-kept secrets.

17 Characteristics of the Clumber Spaniel

Meet the entertaining and affectionate Clumber Spaniel and discover the many endearing characteristics of this rarely seen gundog. This chapter describes the breed's personality and physical traits, including possible health concerns. Are you a worthy Clumber owner?

29 Breed Standard for the Clumber Spaniel

Learn the requirements of a well-bred Clumber Spaniel by studying the description of the breed set forth in the American Kennel Club standard. Both show dogs and pets must possess key characteristics as outlined in the breed standard.

33 Your Puppy Clumber Spaniel

Find out about how to locate a well-bred Clumber Spaniel puppy. Discover which questions to ask the breeder and what to expect when visiting the litter. Prepare for your puppy-accessory shopping spree. Also discussed are home safety, the first trip to the vet, socialization and solving basic puppy problems.

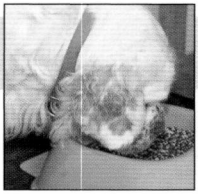

61 Proper Care of Your Clumber Spaniel

Cover the specifics of taking care of your Clumber Spaniel every day: feeding for the puppy, adult and senior dog; grooming, including coat care, ears, eyes, nails and bathing; and exercise needs for your dog. Also discussed are the essentials of dog identification.

Training Your Clumber Spaniel 77

Begin with the basics of training the puppy and adult dog. Learn the principles of house-training the Clumber Spaniel, including the use of crates and basic scent instincts. Get started by introducing the pup to his collar and leash and progress to the basic commands. Find out about obedience classes and training for other activities.

Healthcare of Your Clumber Spaniel 101

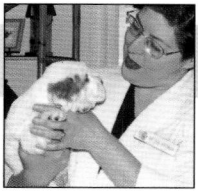

By Lowell Ackerman DVM, DACVD

Become your dog's healthcare advocate and a well-educated canine keeper. Select a skilled and able veterinarian. Discuss breed-specific health concerns, vaccinations and infectious diseases, the neuter/spay decision and parasite control. Also presented is a special section on canine eye disease.

Showing Your Clumber Spaniel 138

Step into the center ring and find out about the world of showing pure-bred dogs. Here's how to get started in AKC shows, how they are organized and what's required for your dog to become a champion. Take a leap into the realms of obedience trials, agility trials, tracking tests and hunting events.

Index 156

Photography by Mary Bloom and Isabelle Français
with additional photographs by:

Alverson Photographers, Ashbey Photography, Baines Photo, Cathy Baker, Ricky Blackman, Robert F. and Jane L. Bonaccorso, Booth Photography, Paulette Braun, Karin Brostam, Gail Budde, Carolina Biological Supply, Debbie Chance, Fritz Clark/The Standard Image, Vicky and Warren Cook, Isabelle Français, Pat Fraser, Walter and Janice Friis, Roe and Gordie Froman, John Hatcher, Carol Ann Johnson, Bill Jonas, Dr. Dennis Kunkel, Kurtis Photography, Tam C. Nguyen, Prof. Dr. Robert L. Peiffer, Jr., Phototake, Jean Claude Revy, Barbara Stebbins and Chuck and Sandy Tatham.

Illustrations by Eileen Heiple and Patricia Peters.

The publisher wishes to thank all of the owners whose dogs are illustrated in this book including Ricky Blackman, Sue Carr, Margaret Curtis, Connie Drake, Leigh Ehrenkrantz, Walter and Janice Friis, John Haenszel, Eileen Heiple, Judith A. Hiller, Douglas Johnson, the O'Neils and Judith and Richard Zaleski.

The author wishes to express special thanks to Roe Froman, DVM, for her excellent work on the health sections of this book. She was kind enough to share with us her particular knowledge as it applies to our breed.

KENNEL CLUB BOOKS® **CLUMBER SPANIEL**
ISBN: 1-59378-224-1

Copyright © 2007 • Kennel Club Books, LLC • 308 Main Street, Allenhurst, NJ 07711 USA
Cover Design Patented: US 6,435,559 B2 • Printed in South Korea

All rights reserved. No part of this book may be reproduced in any form, by photostat, scanner, microfilm, xerography or any other means, or incorporated into any information retrieval system, electronic or mechanical, without the written permission of the copyright owner.

Library of Congress Cataloging-in-Publication Data
Blackman, Ricky.
Clumber spaniel / by Ricky Blackman.
p. cm.
ISBN 1-59378-224-1
1. Clumber spaniel. I. Title.
SF429.C53B53 2006
636.752'4--dc22 2006012321

10 9 8 7 6 5 4 3 2 1

HISTORY OF THE

CLUMBER SPANIEL

The Clumber Spaniel as a distinct breed has been a part of the English canine tradition since the 18th century. Early examples of dogs that looked like Clumber Spaniels have been unearthed in other countries over the years, but no actual independent or coexistent strain has been found in France or elsewhere on the Continent. Therefore fanciers are faced with an intriguing mystery when trying to trace the Clumber Spaniel's actual origin. We do know that the name for the breed came from Clumber Park, the seat of the Duke of Newcastle in the late 18th century. As was the custom with nobles proud of their dogs, he or someone associated with the estate named the breed after his hereditary estate. Though the grand house burned down in 1938, one can still visit the grounds of Clumber Park (which is now part of the UK's National Trust) and find the graves of some of the Clumbers who lived on the estate.

Though the duke and his Clumber Spaniels shared the property, he was probably not responsible for the breed's evolution, or at least there is no

Clumber Spaniels were bred as specialized hunters. This accomplished Clumber is Am./Can. Ch. Jetset's Deke Slayton, showing off his exquisite nose.

definite evidence of that. He is shown in an early painting with dogs that are early specimens of the Clumber Spaniel, but some think that these were dogs that he had been given. Students of the breed have advanced many theories about the origin of this unique dog, but concrete evidence for any one theory is lacking. This perhaps is all for the better—no one likes this kind of good mystery better than a dog lover, and especially a Clumber fancier! And so the debate rages on—people study old pictures, pore over old books for the faintest clues and write back and forth to England and France, looking for evidence, pictures or details that everyone else has missed.

Here is a list of some of the better-known theories regarding the origin of the breed, along with the reasoning behind them:

1. The Clumber is French. Some believe that the breed developed in France and that the Duc de Noailles made a gift of all of his Clumbers to his friend the Duke of Newcastle in the latter part of the 18th century. According to tradition, this was done to save this excellent hunting dog from the perils of the French Revolution. This is the theory to which people subscribed faithfully for quite some time, but it has been rethought as no concrete evidence has been discovered to prove that the breed existed in France at such an early time.

This famous 19th-century painting, *The New Keeper* by C. Burton Barber, depicts the Clumber Spaniel as an avid hunter and lively companion.

2. The Clumber is English (first version). The English aristocracy has always had a great love of hunting. Good dogs were of paramount importance to the sport, and the nobles staffed large kennels on their great estates to breed animals with specialized hunting functions. Several breeds were run in hunting packs and each performed a particular job, such as pointing, flushing or retrieving. In one such kennel—perhaps that of the Duke of Newcastle—an enterprising breeder/kennel manager may have crossed an English spaniel with a Basset

The great English artist Gainsborough painted Madame Lowndestone Norton. The small spaniel in the painting was known as a Clumber, though its resemblance to today's breed is minimal.

Hound. What he got was a superior flushing dog with certain physical characteristics such as extended length and decreased height. Though fine animals such as this were jealously guarded by their owners, it is not unlikely that various noble families exchanged dogs, the interbreeding of which resulted in the very special large white Clumber Spaniel.

An addendum to this theory is that the Clumber worked out so well in England that the dogs were given as highly prized gifts to the French aristocracy. New blood was possibly introduced into the line before they were sent back over to England during the French Revolution to reside at what is now considered to be the breed's ancestral home. Thus we have a French contribution to this eminently English dog. This, of course, makes an especially romantic fairytale.

3. The Clumber is English (second version). In the beginning of the 20th century, the well-known hunting and dog authority James Farrow wrote a monograph on the breed (almost the only book entirely on the breed until quite recently) and theorized that the breed evolved from the larger Blenheim Spaniel. This was a solid hunting dog and also the ancestor of the present-day Cavalier King Charles Spaniel. Farrow examined all of the theories then prevalent and felt that some dogs may have been exchanged as gifts between France and England but that this was originally an English breed.

H. M. The King's Sandringham Spark. H. M. King George V, like his father H. M. King Edward VII, was a great believer in the Clumber Spaniel and had a formidable working dog kennel.

4. The Clumber is Spanish. This theory purports that Clumbers were developed in Spain, gradually evolving from the heavy dog of Navarre into the hunting dog known as the *Pachon*, which is Spanish for "phlegmatic." The Pachon was a calm and even-tempered hunting breed, some of which had long, silky, light-colored coats. It is known that early in the 18th century numerous hunting dogs were imported into England from Spain, but unfortunately the trail goes cold and there is no record of the Pachon being part of those shipments. Enhancing the mystery is the fact that the word "spaniel" does refer to Spain as the origin of a strain of hunting dogs known as Alpine Spaniels.

Whatever the origin, the Clumber Spaniel made its appearance in North America in 1848, first in Canada, and later in the United States. The breed was prized mainly for its hunting ability and was little known to the general public. While Clumber Spaniels were shown in England first in 1859, they were shown in the United States in the latter part of the 19th century. This was only a token representation; however, there was a large enough number of the breed in 1884 for the Clumber Spaniel to be among the first nine breeds recognized by the American Kennel Club. Twenty years later, at the Westminster Kennel Club Dog Show, there were ten dogs entered; that is a typical number of entries still today. Interest in the breed was much more active in England than in the United States during the 19th century because of the patronage of gentry and royalty including Prince Albert, who actually did hunt with the breed.

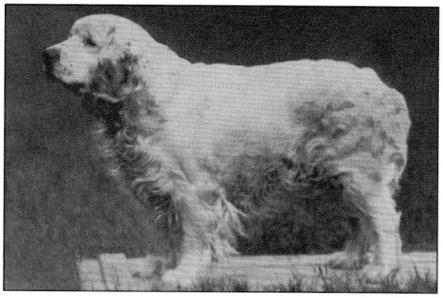

Eng. Ch. Oakerland Repeater, owned by Miss M. F. Reed, is an early 20th-century Clumber Spaniel with a typical head but a relatively short body.

Clumbers were sporadically shown and bred here in the US for the first part of the 20th century. The scene changed in 1930 when Mr. and Mrs. S. Hallock du Pont became the most prominent fanciers of the breed. Mr. du Pont's major interest was hunting; Clumbers were particularly well suited to his type of field work on his estate near Wilmington, Delaware. Of course, these dogs were originally bred to serve as flushing spaniels in the fields of England. There were various packs of dogs, and each hunted with a

A British champion of the 1920s, Eng. Ch. Sir Peter. Modern dogs have a completely different profile and a longer body.

In the early part of the 20th century, Miss Camilla Gurdon, daughter of Lady Cransworth, made a name for herself among British Clumber Spaniel fanciers.

specific purpose, such as pointing the birds' location, flushing them out or retrieving them. An unusual fact is that Mr. du Pont hunted his dogs and bitches separately.

The du Ponts' kennel name was Squirrel Run, which was known for other breeds as well, including English Cocker Spaniels and Labrador Retrievers. Although their original foundation stock was imported from England, especially from Carnforth kennels, Squirrel Run registered approximately 250 dogs over the next 25 years. The du Ponts did have some of their Clumbers shown occasionally so that the dog world could actually see the breed. Their Ch. Squirrel Run Nibble was the first Clumber bitch ever to win a Sporting Group. The beauty of this line of Clumbers can be seen in a series of paintings by Reuben Ward Binks, who also painted many English dogs of various breeds. It is not easy to find a Squirrel Run dog in an extended pedigree today because the du Ponts did not sell their dogs or use them as outside stud dogs, therefore limiting this kennel's impact on the breed. However, their dominance in the breed in those years is impressive for its dedication to their breeding plan, the high quality of their dogs and the dual use of the breed.

This 1890s painting shows a 60-pound Clumber named Lapis, bred by Mr. W. Arkwright, a leading authority on gundogs during the period.

Interest in the breed was kept alive, and its health and longevity improved, by a small dedicated band of breeders and fanciers. In the 1960s this group was led by Eunice Gies, whose kennel name was Andronicus. She and her husband Milton experienced some success in the whelping box and the show ring, especially with her dog Ch. Andronicus Winchester. She was responsible for the creation of the Clumber Spaniel

The original Clumber is shown in this magnificent painting by Francis Wheatley, *Return from Shooting*, in 1788. It depicts the second Duke of Newcastle with the original type of Clumber Spaniel. The painting now hangs in the Sheffield Gallery in the UK.

Club of America (CSCA) in 1972 and was its first president. This club has grown from a founding membership of 44 to a current roster of almost 500. The only founding member still active in the breed is Dr. Bryant Freeman.

In the last few years there has been enough interest in the Clumber Spaniel for the establishment of two local clubs in the Midwest, Williana Clumber Spaniel Club and the Clumber Spaniel Fanciers of Michigan. Both of these clubs offer specialty shows. It is hoped that other parts of the country will gather Clumber enthusiasts together to form their own clubs, to enjoy the fellowship of common interests and to educate the public about the wonderful qualities of the breed.

From the mid-1970s until the early 1990s the major presence in the breed was Betty L. Young from California, a very influential breeder, judge and publicist for the

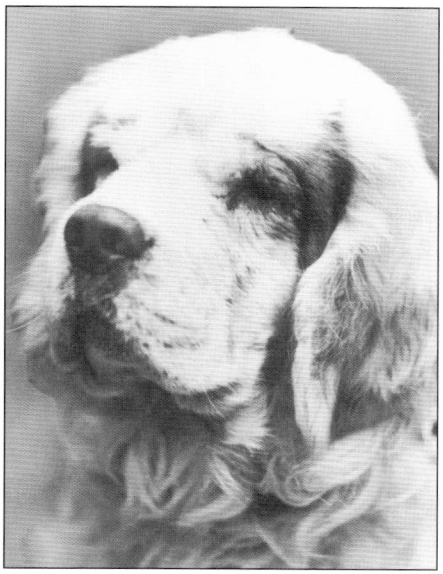

A bit of Clumber history, this photo titled *The Duchess* is from around the time of the turn of the 20th century.

Am./Can. Ch. Smokerise Country Gentleman, owned by Margaret Curtis.

Clumber Spaniel. "Bets," as she was affectionately called by everyone, enjoyed huge success in the show ring, with dogs of her breeding winning the CSCA national specialty six times as well as many Groups and Bests in Show. Many judges all over the US had never seen an example of the breed until they judged Bets's Cypress Woods dogs. Bets and her handler Jo Shellanbarger traveled extensively to shows all over the country, campaigning and winning with her dogs. Her kennel name, Cypress Woods, does appear in many current pedigrees and still has significant impact on today's dogs. We can still look at dogs and recognize a Cypress Woods dog or one that has many ancestors of that line in his background. Bets was most successful in stamping her breeding with its own particular characteristics, which is one of the main goals of any dedicated breeder. When Bets passed away in 1990, we in the US were particularly devastated as we had lost America's own "Mrs. Clumber."

Yes, Clumbers can do a fine job of retrieving, too. Here's Am./Can. Ch. Jetset's Deke Slayton, bringing home the pheasant.

Today the distinction of being the most influential Clumber breeder falls on the capable shoulders of Douglas A. Johnson, a noted breeder and judge who, with his partner, Jeane Haverick, started Clussexx kennels in 1989. This kennel has been successful with both Clumbers and Sussex Spaniels. Douglas handled the first American Clumber to win at England's famed Crufts Dog Show. This was in 2004 with Ch. Clussexx Overdue Bill under noted English breeder/judge Bill Ironside. Doug received the prestigious Sporting Dog Breeder of the Year award for 2005 from the American Kennel Club. Not only have dogs of his breeding won nine national specialties, but Clussexx dogs are the top winners in the breed: the Westminster Best-in-Show-winning male Ch. Clussexx Country Sunrise and the bitch Ch. Clussexx Marry Me Bill. A Clussexx dog is also the sire of the most champions: Ch. Clussexx Billy Goats Gruff, who also won the CSCA national three times. Again the stamp of Clussexx is most recognizable and widespread. It is expected that Mr. Johnson's contribution to and love of the breed will continue far into the future.

WESTMINSTER WINNER

The first Clumber Spaniel to win the United States' prestigious Westminster Kennel Club Dog Show won that honor in 1996: Ch. Clussexx Country Sunrise, owned by Richard and Judith Zaleski and professionally handled by Jane Alston-Myers. "Brady," as he is known, won 13 all-breed Best in Show awards.

A Clumber collectible from the late 1800s/ early 1900s showing an illustration of the breed with the French name "Epagneul de Clumber."

In the last 20 years there have been numerous other qualified, successful and enthusiastic Clumber breeders who have made their marks. These kennels include Sandiam, Critter, Companionway, Cameo, Wicksford, Terryville, Drumhill, Nexus, Breakaway, BlueMoon, Lothian and Woodsman. In a rarer breed such as the Clumber, many dedicated fanciers also contribute their expertise and occasionally breed a wonderful litter; our breed would not be in the healthy state it is in without the combination of

A Clumber Spaniel winning an Award of Merit at the CSCA national specialty. Owner, Janice Friis.

The CSCA works hard to promote and educate the public about their favorite breed. Here are members working at the club's information booth at a Eukanuba/AKC invitational show.

breeders of greater volume and the individuals with only a few dogs.

Over the last ten years Clumber fanciers have broadened their interests, emphasizing the breed's capacity for participating in many types of activities. Historically the function of the breed was hunting, and increasing numbers of fans have been enjoying their days out in the field. Clumber Spaniels also enjoy and excel in obedience, tracking, agility and other performance events. The special bond between dogs and their masters as they work together cannot be overemphasized.

Blazing a trail of success on his way to Westminster Best in Show, Ch. Clussexx Country Sunrise takes Best in Show in 1995 at the Savannah Kennel Club show with handler Jane Alston-Myers.

CHARACTERISTICS OF THE

CLUMBER SPANIEL

It is often heard that one breed or another is "not for everyone." Fortunately, with proper study, a prospective buyer can determine what type of dog is best for him and his own particular living situation. While it is true that every breed has its own individual characteristics, the buyer must know his own characteristics and needs to find what he is looking for in his new canine companion.

PERSONALITY

Clumber Spaniels are "doggy" dogs. This means that they are "in your face" dogs who do not lie in the corner all day and let the world go by. They possess some qualities that may not be desirable for every household, and it is important for you to know about these before you buy the dog. It is better for a breeder to let prospective buyers know about the "bad" or less desirable qualities first. In the Clumber, these qualities include shedding, wet mouths and drooling, back problems and dirtier paws than most dogs. The breed's shedding can be controlled with frequent brushing, and although a Clumber can get wet and muddy and appear to have brown feet, by the time he is dry most of the dirt will have fallen off and he will not even need a bath. However, if a completely neat, hairless house with light-colored rugs or dark-colored furniture is important to you, a Clumber Spaniel is not for you.

This breed, above all, is entertaining. Hardly a moment goes by without some kind of antic, and a Clumber is very upset if his antics are not

Clumber Spaniels are loving, affectionate dogs. Are you ready to accept the love of a "doggy" dog?

Clumbers make handsome and cooperative models. The breed has continued to attract artists through the ages. The rug (pictured below), titled *Clumbers Do It All* and owned by Barbara Stebbins, is by author Ricky Blackman, a rugmaker and designer.

Clumbers at home on their favorite spot—the couch. Many Clumbers snore, but they are so lovable that this minor shortcoming is happily overlooked.

observed by someone and appreciated. Clumbers are lovable and want to express their love every chance they get by kissing you or leaning on you or even attempting to sit on your lap. You can seldom forget there is a Clumber in the room. They snore, but they sleep in such fanciful positions that you laugh when you want to tell them to wake up and stop snoring. Clumbers are people-lovers and sometimes can be overly enthusiastic about greetings, jumping up and wanting to be noticed. Although some would say that dogs cannot feel disappointment or emotions of that kind, if someone walks into a room and does not pay attention to the Clumber, that dog is upset and cannot understand why he is being ignored. It is also a breed characteristic that when they are happy, possibly on just meeting you, they curve their bodies into almost a "U" and wiggle around. Not every Clumber does this, but when you see it, it is charming and you will certainly remember it.

Another characteristic of many Clumbers probably relates to their hunting background. A playful dog may exhibit his joy by picking up the nearest piece of clothing, a towel or another item and carrying it around.

The typical "I am better than you" Clumber look.

Clumber Spaniels make excellent retrieving dogs, especially for bird work. This young Clumber is growing into a top-notch hunting dog.

This can continue for quite some time; the dog does not chew or destroy his prize but simply wants his owner to appreciate his cuteness. Some will not even go outside unless they have something in their mouths.

It is hard to adequately describe the enthusiasm that these dogs have for life and the simple pleasure they bring to their owners. A Clumber's tail will wag every time his owner enters the room as if his owner's presence itself were a gift to the dog. Perhaps this simply is the nature of the dog as a species, that being partners with humans is his ultimate reason for being.

Clumbers are often homebodies who tend to be somewhat lazy. They enjoy sleeping on furniture more than anything else. While they do like to cuddle up and spend time on the sofa, they can be very active and like to play ball, run in your fenced yard, take walks and run around with other dogs and children.

With a common love of the hunt and the Clumber, and a sense of humor, it's the "Old Farts and Feather Fetchers" group. Back row, left to right: Pat Fraser with Neil and Herschel; Sam Catalano with Cleo; Bob Chance with Razzle; Darrell Reeves with Emma, Lollypop and Brutus. Front row, left to right: Linda Fraser with Deke and Torey; Bob Wickwire with Red; Jack Rutherford with Amity; Dick Rusch with Maddie. Five of the dogs pictured are Master Hunters.

This breed can be taught most commands, but a Clumber often will pretend not to hear ones that conflict with his activity (or inactivity) of the moment. Good training practices will work well with Clumbers, as with most breeds, but you will sometimes have to work harder at it.

Most Clumbers would not be described as athletic, but the soundness of the breed has improved greatly in the last 20 years. They can compete in obedience, track enthusiastically and perform their original purpose as hunting dogs in the field. In order to keep your dog trim and healthy, whether he is a pet or show dog, he must be exercised. Walking and playing with the Clumber are good forms of exercise that also allow the owner to spend quality time

Clumbers certainly have a sense of humor!

Author Ricky Blackman with her partner Don Adams and their Clumber and Saluki friends.

with his dog. While the Clumber is a good all-purpose dog, he is happiest with humans, as long as someone is paying attention to him!

Clumber Spaniels were used as hunting dogs on great estates in the 18th and 19th centuries. The dogs were used with other breeds, and each breed had its purpose. The Clumber's original function was as a flushing spaniel. His job was to get the bird into the air after another breed had pointed to the bird's location. Still another breed would retrieve the birds after they were shot, although a Clumber can actually pick up a bird and bring it back quite well. There is a dedicated group of Clumber fanciers who still train their dogs for hunting, and it is hard to tell who enjoys it more—the dogs or the owners!

While most Clumber owners would not feel that the breed can be described as a watchdog, a Clumber will often bark to announce a stranger or a squirrel approaching the house. However, it is very likely that the same dog will welcome that same human visitor into the house with wiggles of pleasure and nudging requests to be petted. A Clumber is not a barking dog and will seldom do so without a reason. The timbre of his bark is lower than that of most dogs, not annoying or ear-piercing at all, and will seem unusual the first time you hear it. A Clumber's bark often sounds as if he is barking with his mouth closed.

Socialization is as important for this breed as any other, and the owner should ensure that the dog meets new people and enjoys new experiences. A dog should be part of the family and take part in as many activities as possible, either at home or away. One of the best ways for a dog to meet new people is to go for walks with his owner through the center of town or other well-populated places. Usually a puppy will attract attention, and a Clumber even more so. Some Clumber puppies will urinate a little bit in their excitement, even at home. This small problem will go away as they get older.

Clumbers are gregarious dogs that get along well with cats and other dogs if they are properly socialized.

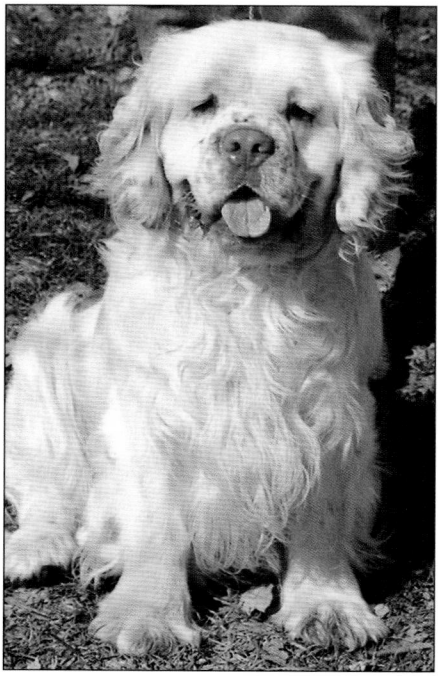

An exuberant and outgoing personality characterizes the smiling Clumber Spaniel.

PHYSICAL CHARACTERISTICS

The first impression of a Clumber is that he is heavier than you expected. The long white hair reminds most people of a short white St. Bernard. The heavy head and somewhat serious expression belie the Clumber's outgoing and exuberant personality. This is a true spaniel with long hairy ears, a full ruff, feathers (long hair) on his front legs and above his hocks and often a flag (long hairs) on his tail. Depending on the country, the tail may be

Clumbers thrive on attention and cuddling, especially from favorite children.

docked or undocked. In many European countries it is now unlawful to dock tails. In the United States the most current standard recognizes both answers to the tail-docking question by stating that docked and undocked tails are of equal value. The breed should have heavy bone, and because of this the dogs weigh more than they appear to. The Clumber is considered a long dog, the height to length proportion being 9 to 11. This breed differs in shape considerably from other spaniels, such as the English Springer. Specimens of this breed can be very good movers, but most have what is known as the "Clumber roll," in which the middle of the back swings somewhat from side to side. This is a breed characteristic and should not throw the dog off his actual movement. It should also not be confused with the roll of an overweight dog. According to the breed standard, a Clumber's particular gait is "comfortable and can be maintained at a steady trot for a day of work in the fields without exhaustion."

Junior aptly illustrates what a good Clumber head looks like.

OWNER SUITABILITY

What kind of owner suits a Clumber best? While all dogs need attention and thrive on their owners' devotion, a Clumber truly blossoms when he is well loved. The more time you give to him, the more devoted he will become. The word "loyal" appears in the standard, but a Clumber is loyal to his owner while his owner is present, and will transfer his love to almost anyone who will give him the time and the care to which he is accustomed. This should not diminish the love that owners feel for their dogs, because looking into the face of

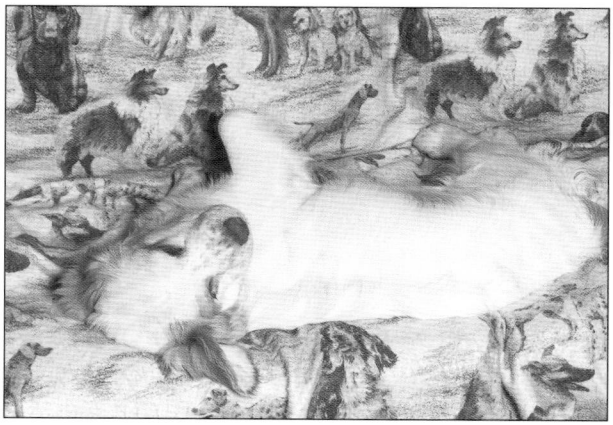

Now here's a dog who knows how to make himself at home!

Children must be instructed to respect the Clumber Spaniel from puppyhood. This young lady and her friends make a lovely portrait.

a Clumber is a pleasure few things can match.

The ideal situation for the happiest Clumber and the happiest owner is a house with easy access to a securely fenced yard, with adequate shade and room to frolic. A Clumber can live in the city in an apartment but will require several good walks a day. The breed enjoys plenty of time outdoors but of equal importance is indoor time with the family.

It cannot be emphasized enough that buying a dog is a commitment; leaving a dog alone for very long periods of time on a regular basis, tying a dog outside or keeping him in the garage or basement are not options in a satisfactory dog household. With any dog, and especially a Clumber, the prospective dog owner must be honest about his reasons for wanting a dog. An ethical breeder should take a dog back if things do not work out, but the animal shelters are full of dogs that were purchased for the wrong reasons and discarded. It is better to think about the possible problems of dog ownership before you get the dog.

The Clumber is a versatile dog, excelling in the field, working well in obedience, showing off in the show ring, learning agility, tracking with vigor and just loving his family.

Clumbers blossom when given a home filled with love.

If you want to be entertained all the time and constantly be the focus of adoring, mischievous eyes, this is the breed for you.

HEALTH CONSIDERATIONS

Clumbers on the whole are healthy, but some consideration must be given to problems that do exist in the breed. Back and neck problems are the conditions that most concern breeders and fanciers. You, as an owner, can use common sense in helping to eliminate situations that may possibly bring on an incidence of a disc problem. It is best not to expect a Clumber to jump down from any high place. A child must never ride on a Clumber's back or attempt anything similar that can endanger those parts of the dog's body.

Clumbers can have eye problems, such as dry eye, that can require prolonged treatment with eye drops. Clumbers in the past have been very prone to hip dysplasia, but with the cooperation of breeders, the incidence of this condition has been decreased. It must be remembered that since this is a rare breed, the gene pool is small and it has been difficult to free the breed of some hereditary conditions. Other problems to discuss with the breeder include immune-mediated hemolytic anemia, hypothyroidism and pyruvate dehydrogenase deficiency.

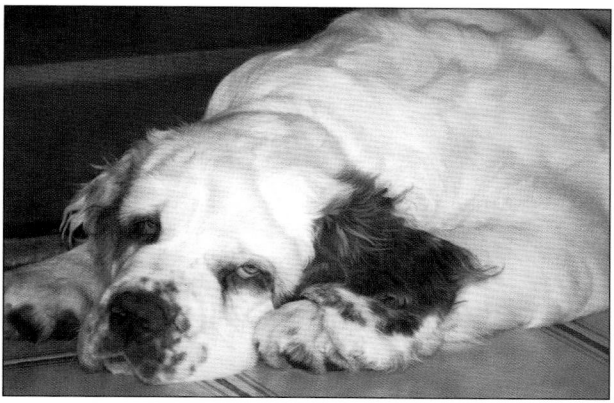

Be certain that the parents of your Clumber puppy have healthy clear eyes.

The small size of the gene pool underlines the importance of finding a reputable breeder, one who pays attention to proper breeding practices, studies the breed and keeps up on the latest medical technology. The buyer of a pet may feel that all of this is not important to him or his dog, but only a healthy dog can be a truly happy one, and the owner will also be happier (and wealthier) if his dog has no health problems and lives a long time.

The life expectancy of a Clumber has lengthened in the last 20 years. If the unpredictable does not happen, you can expect your Clumber to live to be 11 or 12 and sometimes beyond that to 13 or more years, if you are very lucky. The more attention you pay to your dog,

Few dogs are as comical as the Clumber. This gentleman is an expert duck hunter!

and the more you observe him and learn about him, the better you will know when something is wrong and when he needs veterinary attention. Therefore, the healthier he will be and the longer he will live.

It has been stressed, and cannot be stressed enough, that there is a partnership between the dog and the owner. The Clumber brings to this relationship inherent canine qualities with the special characteristics of this particular breed. A dog, however, is somewhat helpless in the human world and cannot provide his own food, shelter or medical care; he must depend on his owner for these tangible things. He must also depend on his owner for the intangible—love. The dog's owner, once he has decided to share his world with a dog, must be willing to live up to this commitment. An investment in a Clumber Spaniel will bring forth much more profit in the form of unconditional, nonjudgmental love than you could have hoped for.

BREED STANDARD FOR THE

CLUMBER SPANIEL

A breed standard is the official description of the way a breed of dog should look and act. Once written and agreed upon, it is the "blueprint" against which breeders and judges evaluate the quality of members of the given breed.

In the United States the breed standard was written by a Clumber Spaniel Club of America committee, approved by its board and voted on by the club membership according to the club's constitution and by-laws. The standard was then accepted by the American Kennel Club and is presented here.

The head of the Clumber Spaniel is a unique feature of the breed; it must be massive and broad on top.

THE AMERICAN KENNEL CLUB BREED STANDARD FOR THE CLUMBER SPANIEL

General Appearance: The Clumber Spaniel is a long, low, substantial dog. His heavy brow, deep chest, straight forelegs, powerful hindquarters, massive bone and good feet all give him the power and endurance to move through dense underbrush in pursuit of game. His white coat enables him to be seen by the hunter as he works within gun range. His stature is dignified, his expression pensive, but at the same time he shows great enthusiasm for work and play.

Size, Proportion, Substance: The Clumber is rectangular in shape possessing massive bone structure and has the appearance of great power. The ideal height for dogs is 18 to 20 inches at the withers and for bitches is 17 to 19 inches at the withers. The ideal length to height is 11 to 9 measured from the withers to the base of the tail and from the floor to the

Head study of correct type, proportion and character.

withers. Dogs weigh between 70 and 85 pounds and bitches weigh between 55 and 70 pounds.

Head: The head is massive with a marked stop and heavy brow. The top skull is flat with a pronounced occiput. A slight furrow runs between the eyes and up through the center of the skull. The muzzle is broad and deep to facilitate retrieving many species of game. The nose is large, square and colored shades of brown, which include beige, rose and cherry. The flews of the upper jaw are strongly developed and overlap the lower jaw to give a square look when viewed from the side. A scissors bite is preferred. The eyes are dark amber in color, large, soft in expression, and deep set in either a diamond shaped rim or a rim with a "V" on the bottom and a curve on the top. Some haw may show but excessive haw is undesirable. Prominent or round shaped eyes are to be penalized. Excessive tearing or evidence of entropion or ectropion is to be penalized. Ears are broad on top with thick ear leather. The ears are triangular in shape with a rounded lower edge, set low and attached to the skull at approximately eye level.

Neck, Topline, Body: The Clumber should have a long neck with some slackness of throat or presence of dewlap not to be faulted. The neck is strong and muscular, fitting into a well laid back shoulder. The back is straight, firm, long and level. The brisket is deep and the ribs well sprung. The chest is deep and wide. The loin arches slightly. The tail is well feathered and set on just below the line of back; its trimming minimal, serving to tidy the feathering to allow for a natural appearance and outline. The tail is normally carried level with the topline or slightly elevated, never down between the rear legs. The tail may be docked or left natural, both being of equal value. If docked, the tail's length should be in keeping with the overall proportion of the adult dog. If natural, the tailbone should extend to the point of hock, but should not extend to the ground.

Forequarters: The Clumber shoulder is well laid back. The upper arm is of sufficient length to place the elbow under the highest point of the shoulder. The forelegs are short, straight and heavy in bone, with elbows held close to the body. Pasterns are strong and only slightly sloped. The front feet are large, compact and have thick pads that act as shock absorbers. Removal of dewclaws is optional.

Hindquarters: The thighs are heavily muscled and, when viewed from behind, the rear is round and broad. The stifle shows good functional angulation, and hock to heel is short and perpendicular to the ground. Lack of angulation is objectionable. The rear feet are not as large or as round as on the front feet but compact, with thick pads and are of substantial size.

Coat: The body coat is dense, straight and flat. It is of good weather resistant texture, which is soft to the touch, not harsh. Ears are slightly feathered with straight hair. Feathering on the legs and belly is moderate. The Clumber has a good neck frill and on no condition should his throat be shaved. Evidence of shaving is to be penalized. The hair on the feet should be trimmed neatly to show their natural outline and for utility in the field. The rear legs may be trimmed up to the point of the hock. Tail feathering may be tidied. Trimming of whiskers is optional.

Ch. Cypress Woods Certified Copy is a good example of proper structure in the Clumber Spaniel.

Color and Markings: The Clumber is primarily a white dog with lemon color or orange color markings. Markings are frequently seen on one or both ears and the face. Facial markings include color around one or both eyes, freckling on the muzzle and a spot on top of the head. A head with lemon/orange markings and an all-white head are of equal

ILLUSTRATIONS OF CORRECT TYPE

value. Freckles on the legs and/or a spot near the root of the tail are also frequently seen and acceptable. The body should have as few markings as possible.

Gait: The Clumber moves easily and freely with good reach in front and strong drive from behind, neither crossing over nor elbowing out. The hocks drive in a straight line without rocking or twisting. Because of his wide body and short legs he tends to roll slightly. The proper Clumber roll occurs when the dog, with the correct proportion, reaches forward with the rear leg toward the centerline of travel and rotates the hip downward while the back remains level and straight. The gait is comfortable and can be maintained at a steady trot for a day of work in the field without exhaustion.

Temperament: The Clumber Spaniel is a gentle, loyal and affectionate dog. He possesses an intrinsic desire to please. An intelligent and independent thinker, he displays determination and a strong sense of purpose while at work. A dog of dignity, the Clumber Spaniel may sometimes seem aloof with people unknown to him, but in time he will display his playful and loving nature. The Clumber Spaniel should never be hostile or aggressive; neither is acceptable and should not be condoned.

CLUMBER SPANIEL

OWNER CONSIDERATIONS

Although the reader of these pages is more likely interested in finding a companionable and family animal than a show prospect, there remain many serious factors governing your choice of a Clumber Spaniel puppy. A primary consideration is time, not only the time of the animal's allotted lifespan, which can be well over 12 years, but also the time required for the owner to exercise and care for the creature. If you are not committed to the welfare and whole existence of this energetic, purposeful animal and if, in the simplest, most basic example, you are not willing to walk your dog daily, no matter what the weather, do not choose a Clumber Spaniel as a companion. Perhaps in that case you are actually not ready for a dog at all, because dogs are living beings whose every need depends on you!

Space is another important consideration. The Clumber Spaniel in early puppyhood may be well accommodated in a corner of your kitchen, but an adult Clumber may weigh up to 85 pounds and will require considerably more space. A yard with a fence is also a basic and reasonable expectation. Most reputable breeders will not sell a dog to a home that does not have a fenced-in yard.

Along with these factors there are the usual issues associated with puppies of any breed, like the damages likely to be sustained by your floors and furniture and, not least of all, restrictions to your freedom, as in vacations or weekend trips. This union is a serious affair and should be considered with family input.

This Clumber puppy is only four weeks of age. Note how beautifully shaped this youngster's head is.

FINDING A QUALIFIED BREEDER

Before you begin your puppy search, ask for references from your veterinarian, other owners and other breeders to refer you to someone they believe is reputable. Responsible breeders usually raise only one or two breeds of dog. Avoid any breeder who has several different breeds or has several litters at the same time. Dedicated breeders are usually involved with a breed or other dog club. Many participate in some sport or activity related to their breed. Just as you want to be assured of the breeder's qualifications, the breeder wants to be assured that you will make a worthy owner. Expect the breeder to interview you, asking many questions about your goals for the pup, your experience with dogs and what kind of home you will provide.

Another option when deciding if you want to add a canine companion, either a Clumber Spaniel or any other breed, to your family, is whether or not you want a puppy. There is a whole world out there of adult dogs available for adoption that may satisfy your needs and fill the empty place in your home more advantageously. You may want to consider a rescue dog, one who needs a good home. The situations that cause rescue dogs to end up in need of new homes vary greatly, among them death of an owner, neglect and myriad other reasons. Prospective adoptive homes are screened to determine their suitability so that the rescue committee can best match up the rescue dogs with good new homes that will meet the dogs' needs and vice versa. If a good fit can be found, the rewards for both the dog and the new owners are so wonderful and satisfying. Most breed clubs, including the CSCA, have active rescue committees that work to place members of their breed with great new owners.

Once you decide to add a puppy or dog to your family, a Clumber Spaniel can be perhaps the most rewarding of all breeds. (Fanciers of each breed will tell you the same thing about their dogs.) A few suggestions will help in buying your dog.

ACQUIRING A PUPPY

The safest method of obtaining your puppy is to seek out a reputable breeder. This is suggested even if you are not looking for a show specimen. The Clumber Spaniel Club of America is a trusted source to refer you to breeders of quality Clumber Spaniels, as are the local Clumber Spaniel clubs.

In this modern age, most canine organizations can be found online, making it easy for you to get in touch with them. The website for the CSCA is www.clumbers.org and provides information about the breed and the club, including contact information for breeder referrals and for breed rescue. It also provides links to other Clumber clubs. It is unlikely that you will find classified ads for Clumber puppies in your local newspaper; if you do, beware. Only obtain a pup or dog from a trusted source.

There are many reasons that you should choose to buy a puppy from a breeder. One of the most important is that a reputable breeder will stand behind his dogs. A breeder may also be an important source of advice and assistance if you have a problem or a question as you raise your Clumber Spaniel. The most reputable breeders are interested in seeing how their extended families turn out.

The breeder spends much time with the young pups, handling them and giving them attention to foster the human-dog bond.

It is seldom that a breeder would sell a puppy before it is at least ten weeks old. A novice dog owner would certainly not be capable of taking care of a younger puppy. The vaccination schedule is very specific and the first shots are certainly the responsibility of the breeder.

A big question for many prospective puppy buyers is the sex of the dog. Many people favor males because they feel them to be more affectionate. If you decide on a female, she should certainly be spayed if she is going to be a pet. This will be better for her future health and much easier for the family. Either sex can and will be an excellent pet if you do your part.

SIGNS OF A HEALTHY PUPPY

Healthy puppies are robust little fellows who are alert and active, sporting shiny coats and supple skin. They should not appear lethargic, bloated or pot-bellied, nor should they have flaky skin or runny or crusted eyes or noses. Their stools should be firm and well formed, with no evidence of blood or mucus.

All of the pups in a Clumber Spaniel litter receive their initial lessons in life from their mother.

If you are convinced that the Clumber Spaniel is the ideal dog for you, it's time to learn what to look for in your search. Since Clumber Spaniels are relatively rare, usually the breeder chooses the puppy he feels is appropriate for your family or for the function that the dog will serve. Many times the breeder will send photos and a video to show you the available pups. Buying a dog of a rare breed is a very different prospect from buying a popular one, which can often be found quite nearby.

Locating a litter of Clumber Spaniels may take some time for the new owner. You should inquire about breeders who enjoy a good reputation in the breed. You are looking for an established breeder with outstanding dog ethics and a strong commitment to the breed. New owners should have as many questions as they have doubts. An established breeder is indeed the one to answer your four million questions and make you comfortable with your choice of the Clumber Spaniel. An established breeder will sell you a puppy at a fair price if, and only if, the breeder determines that you are a suitable and worthy owner of his dogs. An established breeder can be relied upon for advice at any reasonable time. A reputable breeder will accept a puppy back, often without penalty, should you decide that this not the right dog for you.

Choosing a breeder is an important first step in dog ownership. Fortunately, the

NEW RELEASES

Most breeders release their puppies starting at ten weeks of age. A breeder who allows puppies to leave the litter earlier than this may be more concerned with profit than with the puppies' welfare. However, some breeders of show or working breeds may hold one or more top-quality puppies longer in order to evaluate the puppies' career or show potential and decide which one(s) they will keep for themselves.

majority of Clumber Spaniel breeders is devoted to the breed and its well-being. Potential owners are encouraged to attend dog shows to see Clumber Spaniels in action, to meet the handlers firsthand and to get an idea of what Clumbers look like outside a photographer's lens. Provided you approach the handlers when they are not busy with the dogs, most are more than willing to answer questions, recommend breeders and give advice.

When choosing a breeder, reputation is much more important than convenience of location. With the Clumber, prospective owners do not always get the chance to meet the breeder and litter in person, depending on location. In this case, you will have to rely on recommendations, get references and "meet" the breeder and his dogs through phone conversations, e-mail, videos and photos.

Keeping in mind that many top breeders have waiting lists, sometimes new owners have to wait a year or longer for a puppy. If you are really committed to the breeder whom you've selected, then you will wait (and hope for an early arrival!). If not, you may have to go with your second- or

Locating a dam with a nice litter of Clumber Spaniel puppies will require that you do your homework. Contact the Clumber Spaniel Club of America for breeder referrals.

All pups in a litter should be clean, healthy and friendly, and should look like Clumber Spaniels. Whether or not you intend to show your Clumber, you still want a typical representative of the breed.

third-choice breeder. Don't be too anxious, however. If the breeder doesn't have a waiting list, there is probably a good reason.

Once you have contacted (and possibly met) a breeder or two and made your choice about which breeder is best suited to your needs, it's time to visit the litter if feasible. If you do go to a breeder's home to choose your puppy, consider the environment in which the puppies are raised. The puppies should be clean and the pen and area in which they are kept should be as free of feces and other debris as possible. You should take note if there are toys for the puppies and whether they have clean water. If there are

SELECTING FROM THE LITTER

Before you visit a litter of puppies, promise yourself that you won't fall for the first pretty face you see! Decide on your goals for your puppy—show prospect, hunting dog, obedience competitor, family companion—and then look for a puppy who displays the appropriate qualities. You must do thorough research on different breeders so that you feel comfortable with the selecting process. Remember that picking a pet puppy is just as important as picking a show prospect. Your Clumber will be a valued family member and loyal companion for a long time.

scabs, caked dirt or feces on any puppy, or if a pup is matted or has crusty debris in his eyes, common sense should tell you that this puppy has not had the care required to raise a healthy and well-adjusted animal. Do not buy an unhealthy puppy because you are sorry for him, as this will lead to heartbreak.

When visiting a breeder and litter, it is helpful to see the mother and observe her interactions with her puppies and with her owner. In fact, if you do get to see a litter, do not purchase a puppy without first seeing the mother. Sometimes you may get to see the father also, but often the breeder has used a stud dog belonging to another breeder.

You will want to look for an alert puppy, one that is moving around and playing with the others. The puppy should have no tendency to stumble or drag his feet. Look at his mouth to make sure the bite is fairly even, although maturity can correct errors present in puppyhood. If you have any doubt, ask to see the mother's mouth. However, if you are looking for a pet puppy, a mouth that is not totally correct will not be a hindrance in the

Finding a well-bred healthy and sound Clumber puppy will be worth all the effort that you invest.

PEDIGREE VS. REGISTRATION CERTIFICATE

Too often new owners are confused between these two important documents. Your puppy's pedigree, essentially a family tree, is a written record of a dog's genealogy of three generations or more. The pedigree will show you the names as well as performance titles of all dogs in your pup's background. Your breeder must provide you with a registration application, with his part properly filled out. You must complete the application and send it to the AKC with the proper fee. Every puppy must come from a litter that has been AKC-registered by the breeder, born in the US and from a sire and dam that are also registered with the AKC.

The seller must provide you with complete records to identify the puppy. The AKC requires that the seller provide the buyer with the following: breed; sex, color and markings; date of birth; litter number (when available); names and registration numbers of the parents; breeder's name; and date sold or delivered.

dog's life. In fact, sometimes a breeder will sell a dog as a pet rather than a show prospect just because the bite (position of the teeth) is not perfect. With a Clumber you may find that a breeder may offer you a pet puppy with more color than is desirable for the show ring, which of course would not affect your family's enjoyment of the dog at all.

MAKE A COMMITMENT

Dogs are most assuredly man's best friend, but they are also a lot of work. When you add a canine companion to your family, you also are adding to your daily responsibilities for years to come. Dogs need more than just food, water and a place to sleep. They also require training (which can be ongoing throughout the lifetime of the dog), activity to keep them physically and mentally fit and hands-on attention every day, plus grooming and health care. Your life as you now know it may well disappear! Are you prepared for such drastic changes?

Clumber puppies are full of personality and humor. This pup is taking his mom for a walk!

Clumber Spaniels generally have large litters, averaging seven puppies, so selection is good once you have located a desirable litter. Neither the basic structure of the breed nor the temperament has much variation; nonetheless, beware of the shy or overly aggressive puppy and be especially conscious of the nervous Clumber Spaniel pup. Don't let sentiment or emotion trap you into buying a less-than-sound puppy.

Breeders commonly allow visitors to see the litter by around the fifth or sixth week, and puppies leave for their new homes after the tenth week. Breeders who permit their puppies to leave early are more interested in your money than in their puppies' well-being. Puppies need adequate time to learn the rules of the trade from their dams, and they also need to be properly vaccinated before leaving for new homes. Breeders spend significant amounts of time with the Clumber Spaniel toddlers so that they are able to interact with the "other species," i.e., humans. Given the long history that dogs and humans have, bonding between the two species is natural but must be nurtured. A well-bred, well-socialized Clumber Spaniel pup wants nothing more than to be near you and please you.

A COMMITTED NEW OWNER

By now you should understand what makes the Clumber Spaniel a most unique and special dog, one that may fit nicely into your family and lifestyle. If you have researched breeders, you should be able to recognize a knowledgeable and responsible Clumber Spaniel breeder who cares not only about his pups but also about what kind of owner you will be. If you have moved on to the next step in this exciting journey, you have found a litter of quality Clumber Spaniel pups.

Gaining information about and hopefully meeting the puppies and their breeder should be an education in itself. Thorough research is a key aspect of finding the puppy of your dreams. Beyond that, the knowledge you acquire will lay the foundation for a successful future with your pup. Puppy personalities within each litter vary, from the shy and easygoing puppy to the one who is dominant and assertive, with most pups falling somewhere in between. Which type of pup will complement your family dynamics is best determined by observing the puppies in action within their "pack." Whether or not you get to spend time with the pups in person, you will rely on your breeder's expertise and recommendations. Although you may fall in love with a bold and brassy male, the breeder may suggest that another pup would be best for you. The breeder's experience in rearing Clumber

A rare peek at a three-day-old Clumber litter. Obliging our visit is Ch. Critter's Leap of Faith CGC. Breeders don't allow visitors at such a tender age.

GETTING ACQUAINTED

When visiting a litter, ask the breeder for suggestions on how best to interact with the puppies. If possible, get right into the middle of the pack and sit down with them. Observe which pups climb into your lap and which ones shy away. Toss a toy for them to chase and bring back to you. It's easy to fall in love with the puppy who picks you, but keep your future objectives in mind before you make your final decision.

THE FAMILY TREE

Your puppy's pedigree is his family tree. Just as a child may resemble his parents and grandparents, so too will a puppy reflect the qualities, good and bad, of his ancestors, especially those in the first two generations. Therefore it's important to know as much as possible about a puppy's immediate relatives. Reputable and experienced breeders should be able to explain the pedigree, may have pictures of the pup's ancestors to show you and can tell you why they chose to breed from the particular dogs they used.

Spaniel pups and matching their temperaments with appropriate humans offers the best assurance that your pup will meet your needs and expectations. The type of puppy that you select is just as important as your decision that the Clumber Spaniel is the breed for you.

The decision to live with a Clumber Spaniel is a serious commitment and not one to be taken lightly. This puppy is a living sentient being that will be dependent on you for basic survival for his entire life. Beyond the basics of survival—food, water, shelter and protection—he needs much, much more. The new pup needs love, nurturing and a proper canine education to mold him into a responsible, well-behaved canine citizen. Your Clumber Spaniel's health and good manners will

Choosing the right puppy for you is never easy, and having to pick from a litter of adorable Clumber pups makes the decision even harder.

need consistent monitoring and regular "tune-ups," so your job as a responsible dog owner will be ongoing throughout every stage of his life. If you are not prepared to accept these responsibilities and commit to them for the dog's entire lifetime, then you are not prepared to own a dog of any breed.

Although the responsibilities of owning a dog may at times tax your patience, the joy of living with your Clumber Spaniel far outweighs the workload, and a well-mannered adult dog is worth your time and effort. Before your very eyes, your new charge will grow up to be your most loyal friend, devoted to you unconditionally.

Choose your Clumber's water and food bowls wisely. These everyday items should be sturdy enough to endure years of use.

YOUR CLUMBER SPANIEL SHOPPING LIST

Just as expectant parents prepare a nursery for their baby, so should you ready your home for the arrival of your Clumber Spaniel pup. If you have the necessary puppy supplies purchased and in place before he comes home, it will ease the puppy's transition from the warmth and familiarity of his mom and littermates to the brand-new environment of his new home and human family. You will be too busy to stock up and prepare your house after your pup comes home, that's for sure! Imagine how a pup must feel upon being transported to a strange new place. It's up to you to comfort him and to let your little pup know that he is going to be happy with you.

Food and Water Bowls

Your puppy will need separate bowls for his food and water. Stainless steel pans are safer than plastic bowls since they sterilize better and pups are less inclined to chew on the metal. Heavy-duty ceramic bowls are popular, but consider how often you will have to pick up those heavy bowls. Buy adult-sized bowls, as your puppy will grow into them quickly.

The Dog Crate

If you think that crates are tools of punishment and confinement for when a dog has misbehaved, think again. Most breeders and almost all trainers recommend a crate as the preferred house-training aid as well as for all-around puppy training and safety. Because dogs are natural den creatures that prefer cave-like environments, the benefits of crate use are many. The crate provides the puppy with his very own "safe house," a cozy place to sleep, take a break or seek comfort with a favorite toy; a travel aid to house your dog when on the road, at motels or at the vet's office; a training aid to help teach your puppy proper toileting habits; and a place of solitude when non-dog people happen to drop by and don't want a lively puppy—or even a well-behaved adult dog—saying hello or begging for attention.

Crates come in several types, although the wire crate and the fiberglass airline-type crate are the most popular. The wire crates offer better visibility for the pup as well as better ventilation. Many of the wire crates easily collapse into suitcase-size carriers. The fiberglass crates are required for airline travel since they provide more protection for the dog. Fiberglass crates are not recommended for everyday use, though, as they retain the heat and are too "closed-in" for the dogs. Some of the newer crates are made of heavy plastic mesh; they are very lightweight and fold up into slim-line suitcases.

CRATE EXPECTATIONS

To make the crate more inviting to your puppy, you can offer his first meal or two inside the crate, always keeping the crate door open so that he does not feel confined. Keep a favorite toy or two in the crate for him to play with while inside. You can also cover the crate at night with a lightweight sheet to make it more den-like and remove the stimuli of household activity. Never put him into his crate as punishment or as you are scolding him, since he will then associate his crate with negative situations and avoid going there.

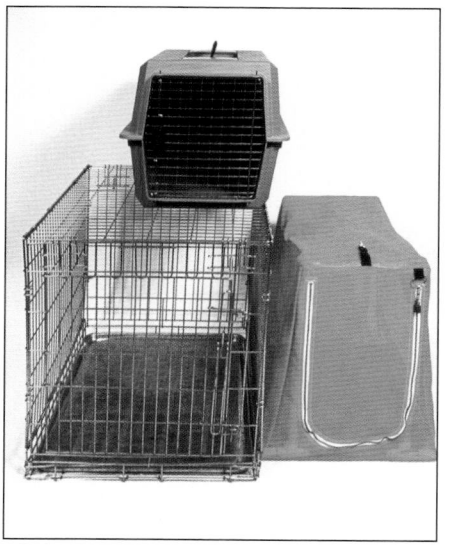

You should be able to find a suitable crate for your Clumber Spaniel at a good pet-supply store.

However, a mesh crate might not be suitable for a pup with manic chewing habits.

Don't bother with a puppy-sized crate. Although your Clumber Spaniel will be a wee fellow when you bring him home, he will grow up in the blink of an eye and your puppy crate will be useless. Purchase a crate that will accommodate an adult Clumber Spaniel. He can stand as tall as about 20 inches at the withers when full-grown, and can weigh up to 85 pounds, so a large-sized crate will be necessary. It is cruel torture for a dog to be in a crate that is too small.

Bedding and Crate Pads

Your puppy will enjoy some type of soft bedding in his "room" (the crate), something he can snuggle into to feel cozy and secure. Old towels or blankets are good choices for a young pup, since he may (and probably will) have a toileting accident or two in the crate or decide to chew on the bedding material. Once he is fully trained and out of the early chewing stage, you can replace

A fiberglass crate with the front door removed can make a cozy den for naptime, but a wire crate is better for confining the dog as it provides better air flow to keep the dog comfortable.

the puppy bedding with a permanent crate pad if you prefer. Crate pads and other dog beds run the gamut from inexpensive to high-end doggie-designer styles, but don't splurge on the good stuff until you are sure that your puppy is reliable and won't tear it up or make a mess on it.

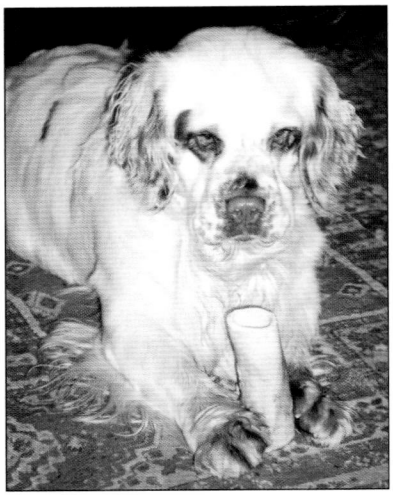

Safe and interesting chew toys will help keep a Clumber happily occupied.

Puppy Toys

Just as infants and older children require objects to stimulate their minds and bodies, puppies need toys to entertain their curious brains, wiggly paws and achy teeth. A fun array of safe doggie toys will help satisfy your puppy's chewing instincts and distract him from gnawing on the leg of your antique chair or your new leather sofa. Most puppy toys are cute and look as if they would be a lot of fun, but not all are necessarily safe or good for your puppy, so use caution when you go puppy-toy shopping.

The best "chewcifiers" are nylon and hard rubber bones, which are safe to gnaw on and come in sizes appropriate for all age groups and breeds. A great toy for an active dog is a football. It is also a good exerciser as the dog will probably kick it and chase after it. You must remember to check all of your dog's toys often to determine if he has started to chew them up. If so, throw them away.

Be especially careful of natural bones, which can splinter or develop dangerous sharp edges; pups can easily swallow or choke on those bone splinters. Veterinarians often tell of surgical nightmares involving bits of splintered bone, because in

Once house-trained, your Clumber will be able to enjoy greater freedom about the house. This Clumber enjoys napping on a big doggie pillow.

addition to the danger of choking, the sharp pieces can damage the intestinal tract. When given to your pup under supervision, however, raw natural marrow bones with most of the marrow removed (it's too rich for a pup) can make an enjoyable and inexpensive toy. Ask the butcher for the ones with the thickest edges, without any splintery pieces on the sides. When the last bit of marrow is gone and the dog has lost interest in it, you can put a piece of cheese or some peanut butter in the middle of the bone, which will keep the dog busy for a while. Only offer this type of bone when you are around to keep an eye on your dog.

Rawhide chews can be dangerous to dogs. Pieces of rawhide are easily swallowed after they get soft and gummy from chewing, and dogs have been known to choke on pieces of ingested rawhide. Never give rawhide to your dog.

Soft woolly toys are special puppy favorites. They come in a wide variety of cute shapes and sizes; some look like little stuffed animals. Puppies love to shake them up and toss them about or simply carry them around. Be careful of fuzzy toys that have button eyes, noses or squeakers that your pup could detach and swallow. Stay away from toys stuffed with sand or chopped foam, both of which will get all

TOYS 'R SAFE

The vast array of tantalizing puppy toys is staggering. Stroll through any pet shop or pet-supply outlet and you will see that the choices can be overwhelming. However, not all dog toys are safe or sensible. Most very young puppies enjoy soft woolly toys that they can snuggle with and carry around. (You know they have outgrown them when they shred them up!) Be careful with toys that have buttons, tabs or other enhancements that can be chewed off and swallowed. Soft toys that squeak are fun, but make sure your puppy does not disembowel the toy and remove (and swallow) the squeaker. Toys that rattle or make noise can excite a puppy, but they present the same danger as the squeaky kind and so require supervision. Hard rubber toys that bounce can also entertain a pup, but make sure that the toy is too big for your pup to swallow.

Growing pups need frequent rest periods in addition to their play periods.

over your home and are not good for your dog, either. Squeaky toys are also popular. Latex squeaky toys do last longer than hard plastic ones, which a Clumber can chew apart in minutes.

Braided rope toys are fun for a dog to chew and toss around, but they shred easily and the strings are easy to swallow. The strings are not digestible and, if the puppy doesn't pass them in his stool, he could end up at the vet's office. Your puppy should be closely monitored with rope toys.

If you believe that your pup has ingested a piece of one of his toys, check his stools for the next couple of days to see if he passes them when he defecates. At the same time, also watch for signs of intestinal distress. A call to your veterinarian might be in order to get his advice and be on the safe side.

An all-time favorite toy for puppies (young and old!) is the empty gallon milk jug. Hard plastic juice containers—46 ounces or more—are also excellent. Such containers make lots of noise when they are batted

about, and puppies go crazy with delight as they play with them. However, they don't often last very long, so be sure to remove and replace them when they get chewed up.

A word of caution about homemade toys: be careful with your choices of non-traditional play objects. Never use old shoes or socks, since a puppy cannot distinguish between the old ones on which he's allowed to chew and the new ones in your closet that are strictly off limits. That principle applies to anything that resembles something that you don't want your puppy to chew.

Learning how to share with other dogs is part of growing up among littermates.

Collars

A lightweight nylon collar is the best choice for a very young pup. Quick-click collars are easy to put on and remove, and they can be adjusted as the puppy grows. Introduce him to his collar as soon as he comes home to get him accustomed to wearing it. He'll get used to it quickly and won't mind a bit. Make sure that it is snug enough that it won't

Collaring Our Canines

The standard flat collar with a buckle or a snap, in leather, nylon or cotton, is widely regarded as the everyday all-purpose collar. If the collar fits correctly, you should be able to fit two fingers between the collar and the dog's neck.

Leather Buckle Collars

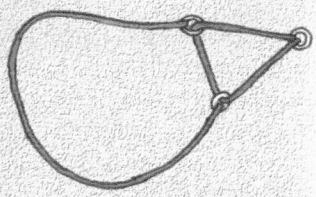

Limited-Slip Collar

The martingale, Greyhound or limited-slip collar is preferred by many dog owners and trainers. It is fixed with an extra loop that tightens when pressure is applied to the leash. The martingale collar gets tighter but does not "choke" the dog. The limited-slip collar should only be used for walking and training, not for free play or interaction with another dog. These types of collar should never be left on the dog, as the extra loop can lead to accidents.

Choke collars, usually made of stainless steel, are made for training purposes but are not recommended for small dogs or heavily coated breeds. The chains can injure small dogs or damage long/abundant coats. Thin nylon choke leads are commonly used on show dogs while in the ring, though they are not practical for everyday use.

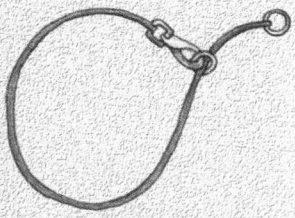

Snap-Bolt Choke Collar

The harness, with two or three straps that attach over the dog's shoulders and around his torso, is a humane and safe alternative to the conventional collar. By and large, a well-made harness is virtually escape-proof. Harnesses are available in nylon and mesh and can be outfitted on most dogs ranging in chest girths of 10 to 30 inches.

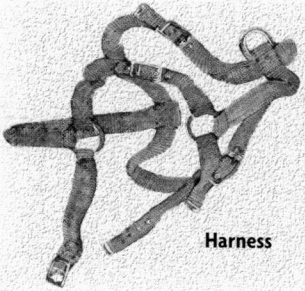

Harness

Nylon Collar

Quick-Click Closure

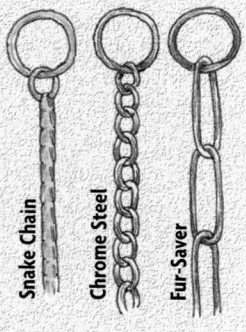

Choke Chain Collars

A head collar, composed of a nylon strap that goes around the dog's muzzle and a second strap that wraps around his neck, offers the owner better control over his dog. This device is recommended for problem-solving with dogs (including jumping up, pulling and aggressive behaviors) but must be used with care.

A training halter, including a flat collar and two straps, made of nylon and webbing, is designed for walking. There are several on the market; some are more difficult to put on the dog than others. The halter harness, with two small slip rings at each end, is recommended for ease of use.

TOXIC PLANTS

Plants are natural puppy magnets, but many can be harmful, even fatal, if ingested by a puppy or adult dog. Scout your yard and home interior and remove any plants, bushes or flowers that could be even mildly dangerous. It could save your puppy's life. You can obtain a complete list of toxic plants from your veterinarian, at the public library or by looking online. It is helpful to have the phone number for poison control, just in case.

slip off, yet loose enough to be comfortable for the pup. You should be able to slip two fingers between the collar and his neck. Check the collar often, as puppies grow in spurts, and his collar can become too tight almost overnight.

Leashes

A 6-foot nylon lead is an excellent choice for a young puppy. It is lightweight and not as tempting to chew as a leather lead. You can switch to a 6-foot leather lead after your pup has grown and is used to walking politely on a lead. For initial puppy walks and house-training purposes, you should invest in a shorter lead so that you have more control over the puppy. At first, you don't want him wandering too far away from you, and when taking him out for toileting you will want to keep him in the specific area chosen for his potty spot.

Once the puppy is heel-trained with a traditional leash, you should consider purchasing a retractable lead. A retractable lead is excellent for exercising adult dogs that are already leash-wise. This type of lead lengthens to allow the dog to roam farther away from you and explore a wider area when out walking, and also retracts when you need to keep him close to you.

HOME SAFETY FOR YOUR PUPPY

The importance of puppy-proofing cannot be overstated. In addition to making your house comfortable for your Clumber Spaniel's arrival, you also must make sure that your house is safe for your puppy before you bring him home. There are countless hazards in the owner's personal living environment that a pup can sniff, chew, swallow or destroy. Many are obvious; others are not. Do a thorough advance house check to remove or rearrange those things that could hurt your puppy, keeping any potentially dangerous items out of areas to which he will have access.

Electrical cords are especially dangerous, since puppies view them as irresistible chew toys. Unplug and remove all exposed cords or fasten them beneath the baseboards where the puppy cannot reach them. Veterinarians and firefighters can tell you horror stories about electrical burns and house fires that resulted from puppy-chewed electrical cords. Consider this a most serious precaution for your puppy and the rest of your family.

Scout your home for tiny objects that might be seen at a pup's eye level. Keep medication bottles and cleaning supplies well out of reach, and do the same with waste baskets and other trash containers. It goes without saying that you should not use rodent poison or other toxic chemicals in any puppy area and that you must keep such containers safely locked up. You will be amazed at how many places a curious puppy can discover!

Once your house has cleared inspection, check your yard. The best way for a puppy to enjoy the outdoors and be safe is to have a fenced pen with gravel or crushed stone on the bottom. There must be access to shade, but a puppy can be left there unattended (with toys) for short periods of time, which can be increased as the puppy gets older. No Clumber should ever be left tied to anything. As for the fence, a 5- to 6-foot-high fence, adequately embedded in the ground to prevent digging under, should be adequate to contain an

TEETHING TIME

All puppies chew. It's normal canine behavior. Chewing just plain feels good to a puppy, especially during the three- to five-month teething period when the adult teeth are breaking through the gums. Rather than attempting to eliminate such a strong natural chewing instinct, you will be more successful if you redirect it and teach your puppy what he may or may not chew. Correct inappropriate chewing with a sharp "No!" and offer him a chew toy, praising him when he takes it. Don't become discouraged. Chewing usually decreases after the adult teeth have come in.

Is there any doubt that this Clumber is a happy dog?

agile youngster or adult. Check the fence periodically for necessary repairs. If there is a weak link or space to squeeze through, you can be sure that a determined Clumber Spaniel will discover it.

The garage and shed can be hazardous places for a pup, as things like fertilizers, chemicals and tools are usually kept there. It's best to keep these areas off limits to the pup. Antifreeze is especially dangerous to dogs, as they find the taste appealing and it takes only a few licks from the driveway to kill a dog, puppy or adult, small breed or large.

VISITING THE VETERINARIAN

A good veterinarian is your Clumber Spaniel puppy's best health-insurance policy. If you do not already have a vet, ask trusted friends and experienced dog people in your area for recommendations so that you can select a vet before you bring your Clumber Spaniel puppy home. Your breeder may even know a vet in your area who is familiar with the breed. Also arrange for your puppy's first veterinary examination beforehand, since many vets do not have appointments available immediately, and your puppy should visit the vet within a day or so of coming home.

It's important to make sure your puppy's first visit to the veterinarian is a pleasant and positive one. The veterinarian should take great care to befriend the pup and handle him gently to make their first meeting a positive experience. The veterinarian will give the pup a thorough physical examination and set up a schedule for vaccinations and other necessary wellness visits. Be sure to show your vet any health and inoculation records, which you should have received from your breeder. Your vet is a great source of canine health information, so be sure to ask questions and take notes. Creating a health journal for your puppy will make a handy reference for his wellness and any future health problems that may arise.

MEETING THE FAMILY

Your Clumber Spaniel's homecoming is an exciting time for all members of the family, and it's only natural that everyone will be eager to meet him, pet him and play with him. However, for the puppy's sake, it's best to make these initial family meetings as uneventful as possible so that the pup is not overwhelmed with too much too soon. Remember, he has just left his dam and his littermates and is away from the breeder's home for the first time. Despite his fuzzy wagging tail, he is still apprehensive and wondering where he is and who all these strange humans are. It's best to let him explore on his own and meet the family members as he feels comfortable. Let him investigate all of the new smells, sights and sounds at his own pace. Children should be especially careful to not get overly excited, use loud voices or hug the pup too tightly. Be calm, gentle and affectionate, and be ready to comfort him if he appears frightened or uneasy.

Be sure to show your puppy his new crate during this first day home. Toss a treat or two inside the crate; if he associates the crate with food, he will

Take precautions around the home so that a snooping Clumber can't stick his nose into danger.

FIRST CAR RIDE

The ride to your home from the breeder might be your puppy's first automobile experience, and you should make every effort to keep him comfortable and secure. Bring a large towel or small blanket for the puppy to lie on during the trip and an extra towel in case the pup gets carsick or has a potty accident. It's best to have another person with you to hold the puppy in his lap. Most puppies will fall fast asleep from the rolling motion of the car. If the ride is lengthy, you may have to stop so that the puppy can relieve himself, so be sure to bring a leash and collar for those stops. Avoid rest areas for potty trips, since those are frequented by many dogs, who may carry parasites or disease. It's better to stop at grassy areas near gas stations or shopping centers to prevent unhealthy exposure for your pup.

This is what life with a Clumber is all about. He is a loved, trusted member of the family who thrives on giving and receiving affection.

associate the crate with good things. If he is comfortable with the crate, you can offer him his first meal inside it. Leave the door ajar so he can wander in and out as he chooses.

FIRST NIGHT IN HIS NEW HOME

So much has happened in your Clumber Spaniel puppy's first day away from the breeder. He has traveled to his new home. He's met his new human family and perhaps other family pets. He has explored his new house and yard, at least those places where he is to be allowed during his first weeks at home. He may have visited his new veterinarian. He has eaten his first meal or two away from his dam and littermates. Surely that's enough to tire out a young Clumber Spaniel pup...or so you hope!

It's bedtime. During the day, the pup investigated his crate, which is his new den and sleeping space, so it is not entirely strange to him. Line the crate with a soft towel or blanket that he can snuggle into and gently place him into the crate for the night. Some breeders send home a piece of bedding from where the pup slept with his littermates, and those familiar scents are a great comfort for the puppy on his first night without his siblings.

He will probably whine or cry. The puppy is objecting to the confinement and the fact that he is alone for the first time. This can be a stressful time for you as well as for the pup. It's important that you remain strong and don't let the puppy out of his crate to comfort him. He will fall asleep eventually. If you release him, the puppy will learn that crying means "out" and will continue that habit. You are laying the groundwork for future habits. Some breeders find that soft

Although the Clumber's sweet expression can melt anyone's resolve, you always must keep in mind that you are the "top dog" in your household.

music can soothe a crying pup and help him get to sleep.

SOCIALIZING YOUR PUPPY

The first 20 weeks of your Clumber Spaniel puppy's life are the most important of his entire lifetime. A properly socialized puppy will grow up to be a confident and stable adult who will be a pleasure to live with and a welcome addition to the neighborhood.

The importance of socialization cannot be overemphasized. Research on canine behavior has proven that puppies who are not exposed to new sights, sounds, people and animals during their first 20 weeks of life will grow up to be timid and fearful, even aggressive, and unable to flourish outside of their familiar home environment.

The eight-to-ten-week-old period is also called the "fear period." This is a serious imprinting period, and the breeder makes sure that all contact during this time is gentle and positive. A frightening or negative event could leave a permanent impression that could affect the puppy's future behavior if a similar situation arises.

Socializing your puppy is not difficult and, in fact, will be a fun time for you both. Lead training goes hand in hand with socialization, so your puppy will be learning how to walk on a lead at the same time that he's meeting the neighborhood. Because the Clumber Spaniel is such a terrific breed, everyone will enjoy meeting "the new kid on the block." Take him for short walks to the park and to other dog-friendly places where he will encounter new people, especially children. Puppies automatically recognize children as "little people" and are drawn to play with them. Just make sure that you supervise these meetings and that the children do not get too rough or encourage him to play too hard. An overzealous pup can often nip too hard, frightening the child and in turn making the puppy overly excited. A bad experience in puppyhood can impact a dog for life, so a pup that has a negative experience with a child may grow up to be shy or even aggressive around children.

Clumber Spaniels love human attention and should adapt relatively quickly to life with their new families.

Take your puppy along on your daily errands. Puppies are

natural "people magnets," and most people who see your pup will want to pet him. All of these encounters will help to mold him into a confident adult dog. Likewise, you will soon feel like a confident, responsible dog owner, rightly proud of your mannerly Clumber Spaniel.

Make sure that your puppy has received his first and second rounds of vaccinations before you expose him to other dogs or bring him to places that other dogs may frequent. Avoid dog parks and other strange-dog areas until your vet assures you that your puppy is fully immunized and resistant to the diseases that can be passed between canines. Discuss safe early socialization with your breeder and vet.

A CRITICAL PERIOD

Canine research has shown that a puppy's 8th through 16th week is the most critical learning period of his life; the importance of this socialization period cannot be stressed enough. This is when the puppy "learns to learn," a time when he needs positive experiences to build confidence and stability. Puppies who are not exposed to different people and situations outside the home during this period can grow up to be fearful and sometimes aggressive. This is also the best time for puppy lessons, since he has not yet acquired any bad habits that could undermine his ability to learn.

LEADER OF THE PUPPY'S PACK

Like other canines, your puppy needs an authority figure, someone he can look up to and regard as the leader of his "pack." His first pack leader was his dam, who taught him to be polite and not chew too hard on her ears or nip at her muzzle. He learned those same lessons from his littermates. If he played too rough, they cried in pain and stopped the game, which sent an important message to the rowdy puppy.

As puppies play together, they are also struggling to determine who will be the boss. Being pack animals, dogs need someone to be in charge. If a litter of puppies remained together beyond puppyhood, one of the pups would emerge as the strongest one, the one who calls the shots.

Fetch is an age-old game between man and dog. Clumbers love to spend time in interactive games with their human companions.

Once your puppy leaves the pack, he will look intuitively for a new leader. If he does not recognize you as that leader, he will try to assume that position for himself. Of course, it is hard to imagine your adorable Clumber Spaniel puppy trying to be in charge when he is so small and seemingly helpless. You must remember that these are natural canine instincts. Do not cave in and allow your pup to get the upper "paw"!

Just as socialization is so important during these first 20 weeks, so too is your puppy's early education. He was born without any bad habits. He does not know what is good or bad behavior. If he does things like nipping and digging, it's because he is having fun and doesn't know that humans consider these things as "bad." It's your job to teach him proper puppy manners, and this is the best time to accomplish that—before he has developed bad habits, since it is much more difficult to "unlearn" or correct unacceptable learned behavior than to teach good behavior from the start.

Make sure that all members of the family understand the importance of being consistent when training their new puppy. If you tell the puppy to stay off the sofa and your daughter allows him to cuddle on the couch to watch her favorite television show, your pup will be confused about what he is and is not allowed to do. Have a family conference before your pup comes home so that everyone understands the basic principles of puppy training and the rules you have set forth for the pup, and agrees to follow them.

The old saying that "an ounce of prevention is worth a pound of cure" is especially true when it comes to puppies. It is much easier to prevent inappropriate behavior than it is to change it. It's also easier and less stressful for the pup, since it will keep discipline to a minimum and create a more positive learning environment for him. That, in turn, will also be easier on you!

Here are a few commonsense tips to keep your belongings safe and your puppy out of trouble:

- Keep your closet doors closed and your shoes, socks and other apparel off the floor so

Treats make lesson time more interesting to the Clumber, who sometimes can be a challenge to train.

This foursome enjoys some socialization time outdoors in the fresh air and sunshine.

your puppy can't get at them.

- Keep a secure lid on the trash container or put the trash where your puppy can't dig into it. He can't damage what he can't reach!
- Supervise your puppy at all times to make sure he is not getting into mischief. If he starts to chew the corner of the rug, you can distract him instantly by tossing a toy for him to fetch. You also will be able to whisk him outside when you notice that he is about to piddle on the carpet. If you can't see your puppy, you can't teach him or correct his behavior.

SOLVING PUPPY PROBLEMS

Chewing and Nipping

Nipping at fingers and toes is normal puppy behavior. Chewing is also the way that puppies investigate their surroundings. However, you will have to teach your puppy that chewing anything other than his toys is not acceptable. That won't happen overnight and at times puppy teeth will test your patience. However, if you allow nipping and chewing to continue, just think about the damage that a mature Clumber Spaniel can do with a full set of adult teeth.

Whenever your puppy nips your hand or fingers, cry out "Ouch!" in a loud voice, which should startle your puppy and stop him from nipping, even if only for a moment. Immediately distract him by offering a small treat or an appropriate toy for him to chew instead (which means having chew toys and puppy treats handy or in your pockets at all times). Praise him when he takes the toy and tell him what a good fellow he is. Praise is just as or even more important in puppy training as discipline and correction.

Puppies also tend to nip at children more often than adults, since they perceive little ones to

REPEAT YOURSELF

Puppies learn best through repetition. Use the same verbal cues and commands when teaching your puppy new behaviors or correcting for misbehaviors. Be consistent, but not monotonous. Puppies get bored just like puppy owners.

be more vulnerable and more similar to their littermates. Teach your children appropriate responses to nipping behavior. If they are unable to handle it themselves, you may have to intervene. Puppy nips can be quite painful and a child's frightened reaction will only encourage a puppy to nip harder, which is a natural canine response. As with all other puppy situations, interaction between your Clumber Spaniel puppy and children should be supervised.

Chewing on objects, not just family members' fingers and ankles, is also normal canine behavior that can be especially tedious (for the owner, not the pup) during the teething period when the puppy's adult teeth are coming in. At this stage, chewing just plain feels good. Furniture legs and cabinet corners are common puppy favorites. Shoes and other personal items also taste pretty good to a pup.

The best solution is, once again, prevention. If you value something, keep it tucked away and out of reach. You can't hide your dining-room table in a closet, but you can try to deflect the chewing by applying a bitter product made just to deter dogs from chewing. This spray-on substance is vile-tasting, although safe for dogs, and most puppies will avoid the forbidden object after one tiny taste. You also can apply the product to your leather leash if the puppy tries to chew on it.

KEEP OUT OF REACH

Most dogs don't browse around your medicine cabinet, but accidents do happen! The drug acetaminophen, the active ingredient in Tylenol®, can be deadly to dogs and cats if ingested in large quantities. Acetaminophen toxicity, caused by the dog's swallowing 15 to 20 tablets, can be manifested in abdominal pains within a day or two of ingestion, as well as liver damage. If you suspect your dog has swiped a bottle of Tylenol®, get the dog to the vet immediately so that the vet can induce vomiting and cleanse the dog's stomach.

Keep a ready supply of safe chews handy to offer your Clumber Spaniel as a distraction when he starts to chew on something that's a "no-no." Remember, at this tender age, he does not yet know what is permitted or forbidden, so you have to be "on call" every minute he's awake and on the prowl.

You may lose a treasure or two during puppy's growing-up period, and the furniture could sustain a nasty nick or two. These can be trying times, so be prepared for those inevitable accidents and comfort yourself in knowing that this too shall pass.

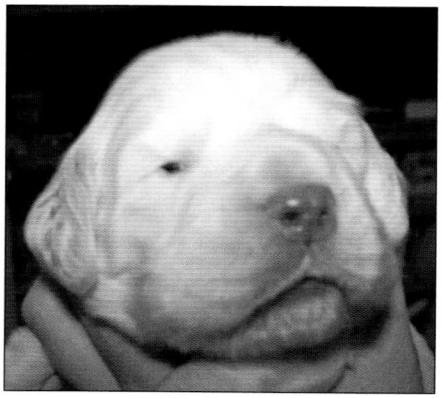

A tiny Clumber puppy, just a few days in this world. This pup has a lot of growing to do and needs good care and guidance every step of the way.

Puppy Whining

Puppies often cry and whine, just as infants and little children do. It's their way of telling us that they are lonely or in need of attention. Your puppy will miss his littermates and will feel insecure when he is left alone. You may be out of the house or just in another room, but he will still feel alone. During these times, the puppy's crate should be his personal comfort station, a place all his own where he can feel safe and secure. Once he learns that being alone is okay and not something to be feared, he will settle down without crying or objecting. You might want to leave a radio on while he is crated, as the sound of human voices can be soothing and will give the impression that people are around.

Give your puppy a favorite cuddly toy or chew toy to entertain him whenever he is crated. You will both be happier: the puppy because he is safe in his den and you because he is quiet, safe and not getting into puppy escapades that can wreak havoc in your house or cause him danger.

To make sure that your puppy will always view his crate as a safe and cozy place, never, *ever* use the crate as punishment. That's the best way to turn the crate into a negative place that the pup will want to avoid. Sure, you can use the crate for your own peace of mind if your puppy is getting into trouble and needs some "time out." Just don't let him know that! Never scold the pup and immediately place him into the crate. Count to ten, give him a couple of hugs and maybe a treat, then scoot him into his crate.

It's also important not to make a big fuss when he is released from the crate. That will make getting out of the crate more appealing than being in the crate, which is just the opposite of what you are trying to achieve.

Who can resist these faces? The Clumber's appeal and charm are undeniable in pups and adults alike.

PROPER CARE OF YOUR

CLUMBER SPANIEL

Adding a Clumber Spaniel to your household means adding a new family member who will need your care each and every day. When your Clumber Spaniel pup first comes home, you will start a routine with him so that, as he grows up, your dog will have a daily schedule just as you do. The aspects of your dog's daily care will likewise become regular parts of your day, so you'll both have a new schedule. Dogs learn by consistency and thrive on routine: regular times for meals, exercise, grooming and potty trips are just as important for your dog as they are for you! Your dog's schedule will depend much on your family's daily routine, but remember that you now have a new member of the family who is part of your day every day.

FEEDING

Feeding your dog the best diet is based on various factors, including age, activity level, overall condition and size of breed. When you visit the breeder, he will share with you his advice about the proper diet for your dog based on his experience with the breed and the foods with which he has had success. Likewise, your vet will be a helpful source of advice throughout the dog's life and will aid you in planning a diet for optimal health.

Feeding the Puppy

Of course, your pup's very first food will be his dam's milk. There may be special situations in which pups fail to nurse, necessitating that the breeder hand-feed them with a formula, but for the most part pups spend the first weeks of life nursing from their dam. The breeder weans the pups by gradually introducing solid foods and decreasing the milk meals. Pups may even start themselves off on the weaning process, albeit inadvertently, if they snatch bites from their mom's food bowl.

Puppies should be allowed to nurse for three to four weeks and should be slowly weaned away from their mother by introducing small portions of raw chopped meat, cereal and canned milk. By the time they are six weeks old,

Mother's milk offers the best start in life for pups as it gives them the nutrients that they need and immunity from disease before they are vaccinated.

they should be completely weaned and fed solely a dry puppy food. Dry puppy food should always be soaked in boiling water so that it is soft enough for the puppy to eat until he gets his adult teeth.

During the weaning period, the diet is most important as puppies grow fastest during the first year of life. It has been determined by knowledgeable and experienced Clumber Spaniel breeders that puppy food should not be given after three to four months of age because it encourages the heavier breeds like the Clumber to grow more quickly. It is strongly recommended that adult food be given at this time. The dog will attain his proper size, but at a slower and healthier rate. Some Clumber breeders do not give puppy food at all.

Feeding the pup at the same times and in the same place each day is important for both housebreaking purposes and establishing the dog's everyday routine. Clumbers up to eight weeks of age should be fed four times a day, then three times a day until four to six months old and then twice a day throughout their lives. It is healthier to divide the food into two daily meals rather than one large daily portion.

SWITCHING FOODS

There are certain times in a dog's life when it becomes necessary to switch his food; for example, from puppy to adult food and then from adult to senior-dog food. Additionally, you may decide to feed your pup a different type of food from what he received from the breeder, and there may be "emergency" situations in which you can't find your dog's normal brand and have to offer something else temporarily. Anytime a change is made, for whatever reason, the switch must be done gradually. You don't want to upset the dog's stomach or end up with a picky eater who refuses to eat something new. A tried-and-true approach is, over the course of about a week, to mix a little of the new food in with the old, increasing the proportion of new to old as the days progress. At the end of the week, you'll be feeding his regular portions of the new food, and he will barely notice the change.

VARIETY IS THE SPICE

Although dog-food manufacturers contend that dogs don't like variety in their diets, studies show quite the opposite to be true. Dogs would much rather vary their meals than eat the same old chow day in and day out. Dry kibble is no more exciting for a dog than the same bowl of bran flakes would be for you. Fortunately, there are dozens of varieties available on the market, and your dog will likely show preference for certain flavors over others. A word of warning: don't overdo it or you'll develop a fussy eater who only prefers chopped beef fillet and asparagus tips every night.

Puppy diets should be balanced for your dog's needs, and supplements of vitamins, minerals and protein should not be necessary and can even be dangerous. As for the amount to feed, a pup should never be allowed to gain excess weight. Dogs of all ages should be kept in proper body condition, but extra weight can strain a pup's developing frame, causing skeletal problems.

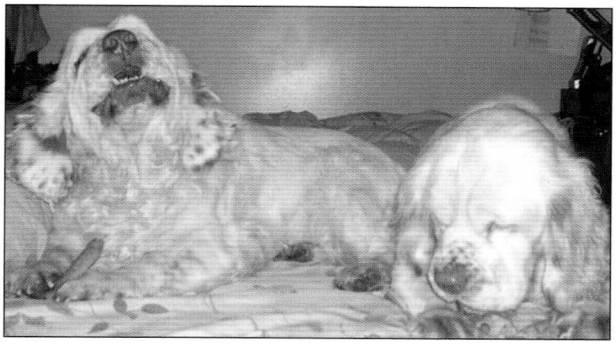

Healthy treats! Crunchy carrots are good for a dog's teeth, provide nutrition and don't add unnecessary calories...and are just plain fun to eat.

Watch your pup's weight as he grows and, if the recommended amounts seem to be too much or too little for your pup, consult the vet about appropriate dietary changes. Keep in mind that treats, although small, can quickly add up throughout the day, contributing unnecessary calories. Treats are fine when used prudently; opt for dog treats specially formulated to be healthy or for nutritious snacks like small pieces of cheese or cooked chicken.

A good adult-formula dog food in proper amounts should maintain your Clumber in good health and condition.

Feeding the Adult Dog

For the adult (meaning physically mature) dog, feeding properly is about maintenance, not growth. A

Where food is concerned, a Clumber Spaniel must be taught that he is not allowed to help himself.

Clumber Spaniel reaches adulthood at about two years of age, and true maturity at about five years old, but is started on an adult food much earlier, around three or four months old. Again, correct weight is a concern. Your dog should appear fit and should have an evident "waist." His ribs should not be protruding (a sign of being underweight), but they should be covered by only a slight layer of fat. Under normal circumstances, an adult dog can be maintained fairly easily with a high-quality nutritionally complete adult-formula food.

Factor treats into your dog's overall daily caloric intake, and avoid offering table scraps. Not only are certain "people" foods, like chocolate, nuts, grapes, raisins, onions and significant quantities of garlic, toxic to dogs but feeding from your plate also encourages begging and overeating. Overweight dogs are more prone to health problems. Research has even shown that obesity takes years off a dog's life. With that in mind, resist the urge to overfeed and over-treat. Don't make unnecessary additions to your dog's diet, whether with tidbits or with extra vitamins and minerals.

The amount of food needed for proper maintenance will vary depending on the individual dog's activity level, but you will be able to tell whether the daily portions are keeping him in good shape. With the wide variety of good complete foods available, choosing what to feed is largely a matter of personal preference. Just as with the puppy, the adult dog should have consistency in his mealtimes and feeding place. In addition to a consistent routine, regular mealtimes also allow the owner to see how much his dog is eating. If the dog seems never to be satisfied or, likewise, becomes uninterested in his food, the owner will know right away that something is wrong and can consult the vet. With a regular schedule, a dog can also be given some quiet time before and after meals, which is healthy for all dogs.

Diets for the Aging Dog

A good rule of thumb is that once a dog has reached around 75% of his expected lifespan, he has reached "senior citizen" or geriatric status. What does aging have to do with your dog's diet? No, he won't get a discount at the local diner's early-bird special. Yes, he may require some dietary changes to accommodate the changes that come along with increased age. One change is that the older dog's dietary needs become more similar to that of a puppy. Specifically, dogs can metabolize more protein as youngsters and seniors than in the adult-maintenance stage. Discuss with your vet whether you need to switch to a higher-protein or senior-formulated food or whether your current adult-dog food contains sufficient nutrition for the senior. With Clumbers, it's often unnecessary to make a switch unless there is a health- or age-related problem. Many do fine on regular adult dog food in their senior years.

Watching the dog's weight remains essential, even more so in the senior stage. Older dogs are already more vulnerable to illness, and obesity only contributes to their susceptibility to problems. As the older dog becomes less active and thus exercises less, his regular portions may cause him to gain weight. At this point, you may consider decreasing his daily food intake or switching to a reduced-calorie food. As with other changes, you should consult your vet for advice.

Don't Forget the Water!

For a dog, it's always time for a drink! Regardless of what type of food he eats, there's no doubt that he needs plenty of water. Fresh cold water, in a clean bowl,

DIET DON'TS

- Got milk? Don't give it to your dog! Dogs cannot tolerate large quantities of cows' milk, as they do not have the enzymes to digest lactose.
- You may have heard of dog owners who add raw eggs to their dogs' food for a shiny coat or to make the food more palatable, but consumption of raw eggs too often can cause a deficiency of the vitamin biotin.
- Avoid feeding table scraps, as they will upset the balance of the dog's complete food. Additionally, fatty or highly seasoned foods can cause upset canine stomachs.
- Do not offer raw meat to your dog. Raw meat can contain parasites; it also is high in fat.
- Vitamin A toxicity in dogs can be caused by too much raw liver, especially if the dog already gets enough vitamin A in his balanced diet, which should be the case.
- Bones like chicken, pork chop and other soft bones are not suitable, as they easily splinter.

QUENCHING HIS THIRST

Is your dog drinking more than normal and trying to lap up everything in sight? Excessive drinking has many different causes. Obvious causes for a dog's being thirstier than usual are hot weather and vigorous exercise. However, if your dog is drinking more for no apparent reason, you could have cause for concern. Serious conditions like kidney or liver disease, diabetes and various types of hormonal problems can all be indicated by excessive drinking. If you notice your dog's being excessively thirsty, contact your vet at once. Hopefully there will be a simpler explanation, but the earlier a serious problem is detected, the sooner it can be treated, with a better rate of cure.

should be freely available to your dog at all times. There are special circumstances, such as during puppy housebreaking, when you will want to monitor your pup's water intake so that you will be able to predict when he will need to relieve himself, but water must be available to him nonetheless. Water is essential for hydration and proper body function just as it is in humans.

You will get to know how much your dog typically drinks in a day. Of course, in the heat or if exercising vigorously, he will be more thirsty and will drink more. However, if he begins to drink noticeably more water for no apparent reason, this could signal any of various problems, and you are advised to consult your vet.

Water is the best drink for dogs. Some owners are tempted to give milk from time to time or to moisten dry food with milk, but dogs do not have the enzymes necessary to digest the lactose in milk, which is much different from the milk that nursing puppies receive. Therefore stick with clean fresh water to quench your dog's thirst, and always have it readily available to him.

EXERCISE

We all know the importance of exercise for humans, so it should come as no surprise that it is

Once your Clumber is well trained on leash, all members of the family can share the responsibility for his daily walks.

essential for our canine friends as well. The Clumber Spaniel is a moderately active dog. While it seems that a Clumber would rather lie on the sofa, he does need, enjoy and benefit from regular exercise. Now, regardless of your own level of fitness, get ready to assume the role of personal trainer for your dog. It's not as hard as it sounds, and it will have health benefits for you, too.

Just as with anything else you do with your dog, you must set a routine for his exercise. It's the same as your daily morning run before work or never missing the 7 p.m. aerobics class. If you plan it and get into the habit of actually doing it, it will become just another part of your day. Think of it as making daily exercise appointments with your dog, and stick to your schedule.

As a rule, dogs in normal health should have at least a half-hour of activity each day. Dogs with health or orthopedic problems may have specific limitations, so their exercise plans are best devised with the help of a vet. For healthy dogs, there are many ways to fit 30 minutes of activity into your day. Depending on your schedule, you may plan a 15-minute walk or activity session in the morning and again in the evening, or do it all at once in a half-hour session each day. Walking is the most

Your Clumber needs exercise as much as you do for a fit body and mind.

popular way to exercise a dog (it's good for you, too!); other suggestions include retrieving games, disc-catching or other active games with his toys. If you have a safe body of water nearby and a dog that likes to swim, swimming is an excellent form of exercise for dogs, putting no stress on his frame. Some Clumbers really do enjoy the water; you will know if yours likes to swim if he takes to water voluntarily.

On that note, some precautions should be taken with a puppy's exercise. During his first year, when he is doing most of his growing and developing, your Clumber Spaniel should not be subject to stressful activity that stresses his body. Short walks at a comfortable pace and play sessions in the yard are good for a growing pup, and his exercise can be increased as he grows up.

For overweight dogs, dietary changes and activity will help the goal of weight loss. (Sound familiar?) While they should of course be encouraged to be active, remember not to overdo it, as the excess weight is already putting strain on his vital organs and bones. As for more active dogs, some of them never seem to tire! All Clumbers enjoy time spent with their owners, doing things together.

Regardless of your dog's condition and activity level, exercise offers benefits to all dogs and owners. Consider the fact that dogs who are kept active are more stimulated both physically and mentally, meaning that they are less likely to become bored and lapse into destructive behavior. Also consider the benefits of one-on-one time with your dog every day, continually strengthening the bond between the two of you. Furthermore, exercising together will improve health and longevity for both of you. You both need exercise, and now you and your dog have a workout partner and motivator!

The outdoors can be damaging to a dog's feet, even those with thick pads like the Clumber's. You should check your Clumber's feet after time spent outdoors.

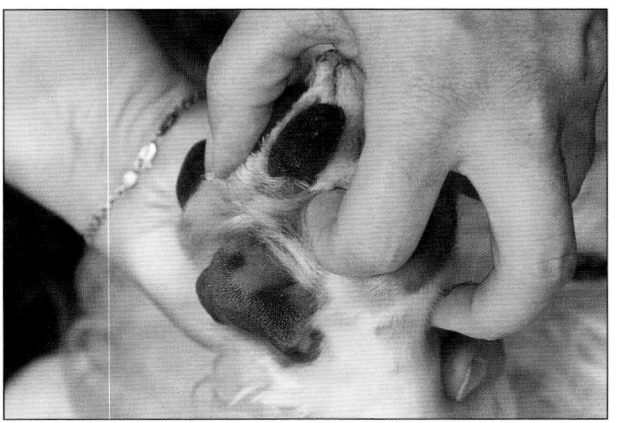

GROOMING

Brushing

Clumber Spaniels do not require extensive grooming, as they are considered a natural dog. A pin brush or a metal rake can be used for routine brushing. Brush the coat several times a week to remove dead hair and stimulate the dog's natural oils, adding shine and a healthy look to the coat. Brush more in those places where the hair is the longest. Your regular grooming sessions are a good way to spend time with your dog. Many dogs grow to like the feel of being brushed and will enjoy the routine.

Clumber Spaniels should never have their necks shaved as some spaniels do. Their feet should be tidied and the hair on their foot pads should be trimmed. You should also check that there are no stones or mats between the pads of their feet to hinder their walking. You may also want to trim the hair under their ears, as that is the first place that mats. Under the front elbows is another place that mats easily. You should also check the hair above the hocks, as this mats often as well, and make sure there are no feces stuck in the coat under the tail.

Bathing

In general, dogs need to be bathed only a few times a year, possibly more often if your dog gets into something messy or if he starts to smell like a dog. Show dogs are bathed more often, sometimes before every show, although this depends on the owner. Bathing too frequently can have negative effects on the skin and coat, removing natural oils and causing dryness.

If you give your dog his first bath when he is young, he will become accustomed to the process. Wrestling a dog into the tub or chasing a freshly shampooed dog who has escaped from the bath will be no fun! Most dogs don't naturally enjoy their baths, but you at least want yours to cooperate with you.

Before bathing the dog, have the items you'll need close at hand. First, decide where you will bathe the dog. You should have a tub or basin with a non-slip surface. Puppies can even be bathed in a sink. In warm weather, some like to use a portable pool in the yard, although you'll want to make sure your dog doesn't head for the nearest dirt pile following his bath! You will also need a hose or shower spray to wet the coat thoroughly, a shampoo formulated for dogs, absorbent towels and a blow dryer. Human shampoos are too harsh for dogs' coats and will dry them out.

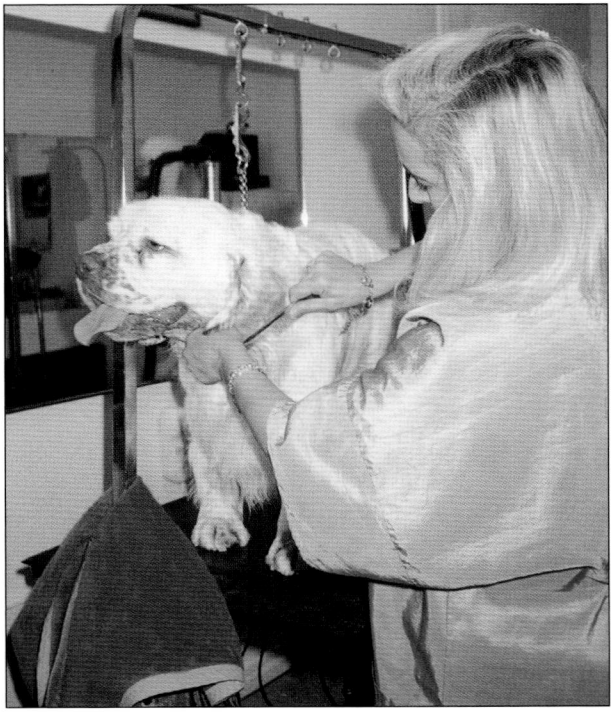

Professionals use a grooming table to keep the dog standing in place and at a height that is comfortable to work with. Some owners like to use these at home as well.

Before wetting the dog, give him a brush-through to remove any dead hair, dirt and tangles. The feathering should be combed out to make sure there are no mats. Make sure that your Clumber is at ease in the tub and have the water at a comfortable temperature. Begin bathing by wetting the coat all the way down to the skin. Massage in the shampoo, keeping it away from his face and eyes. Rinse him thoroughly, again avoiding the eyes and ears, as you don't want to get water into the ear canals. A thorough rinsing is important, as shampoo residue is drying and itchy to the dog. You should use a canine coat conditioner after the shampoo has been rinsed away. Using conditioner at the end of the bath not only helps to remove tangles but also helps to prevent them. After rinsing out the conditioner, wrap him in a towel to absorb the initial moisture. Gently towel-dry, being careful not to create tangles, and then finish with a blow dryer on low heat, held at a safe distance from the dog and brushing as you dry. You should keep the dog indoors and away from drafts until he is completely dry.

Nail Clipping

Having their nails trimmed is not on many dogs' lists of favorite things to do. With this in mind, you will need to accustom your puppy to the procedure at a young age so that he will sit still (well, as still as he can) for his pedicures. Long nails can cause the dog's feet to spread, which is not good for him; likewise, long nails can hurt if they unintentionally scratch, not good for you!

Some dogs' nails are worn down naturally by regular walking on hard surfaces, so the frequency with which you clip depends on your individual dog. Look at his nails from time to time and clip as needed; a good

WATER SHORTAGE

No matter how well behaved your dog is, bathing is always a project! Nothing can substitute for a good warm bath, but owners do have the option of giving their dogs "dry" baths. Pet shops sell excellent products, in both powder and spray forms, designed for spot-cleaning your dog. These dry shampoos are convenient for touch-up jobs when you don't have the time to bathe your dog in the traditional way.

Muddy feet, messy behinds and smelly coats can be spot-cleaned and deodorized with a "wet-nap"-style cleaner. On those days when your dog insists on rolling in fresh goose droppings and there's no time for a bath, a spot bath can save the day. These pre-moistened wipes are also handy for other grooming needs like wiping faces, ears and eyes and freshening tails and behinds.

Regular grooming and bathing as needed will keep your Clumber looking and smelling clean, and more pleasant to share your sofa with!

way to know when it's time for a trim is if you hear your dog clicking as he walks across the floor. If your dog has dewclaws, do not forget to clip them, as they do not wear down and can grow around and into the leg.

There are several types of nail clippers and even electric nail-grinding tools made for dogs; first we'll discuss using the clipper. To start, have your clipper ready and some doggie treats on hand. You want your pup to view his nail-clipping sessions in a positive light, and what better way to convince him than with food? You may want to enlist the help of an assistant to comfort the pup and offer treats as you concentrate on the clipping itself. The guillotine-type clipper is thought of by many as the easiest type to use; the nail tip is inserted into the opening, and blades on the top and bottom snip it off in one clip.

Start by grasping the pup's paw; a little pressure on the foot pad causes the nail to extend, making it easier to clip. Clip off a little at a time. If you can see the "quick," which is a blood vessel that runs through each nail, you will know how much to trim, as you do not want to cut into the quick. On that note, if you do cut the quick, which will cause bleeding, you can stem the flow of blood with a styptic pencil or

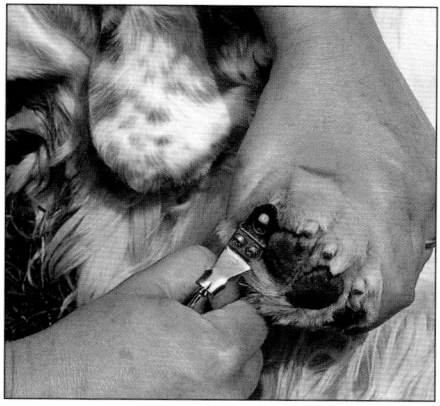

Use a guillotine-style nail clipper to trim your Clumber's nails. It can be purchased at your local pet-supply shop.

other clotting agent. If you mistakenly nip the quick, do not panic or fuss, as this will cause the pup to be afraid. Simply reassure the pup, stop the bleeding and move on to the next nail. Don't be discouraged; you will become a professional canine pedicurist with practice.

You may or may not be able to see the quick, so it's best to just clip off a small bit at a time. If you see a dark dot in the center of the nail, this is the quick and your cue to stop clipping. Tell the puppy he's a "good boy" and offer a piece of treat with each nail. You can also use nail-clipping time to examine the footpads, making sure that they are not dry and cracked and that nothing has become embedded in them.

The nail grinder, the other choice, is many owners' first choice. Accustoming the puppy to the sound of the grinder and

Along with the sunshine and soft green grass, the warm weather also ushers in the flea season. Closely examine your Clumber's coat after he's been outdoors.

sensation of the buzz presents fewer challenges than the clipper, and there's no chance of cutting through the quick, although you do have to be careful not to catch any of the leg hair in the grinder. Use the grinder on a low setting and always talk soothingly to your dog. He won't mind his salon visit, and he'll have nicely polished nails as well.

Ear Cleaning

While keeping your dog's ears clean unfortunately will not cause him to "hear" your commands any better, it will protect him from ear infection and ear-mite infestation. In addition, a dog's ears are vulnerable to waxy build-up and to collecting foreign matter from the outdoors. Look in your dog's ears regularly to ensure that they look pink, clean and otherwise healthy. Even if they look fine, an odor in the ears signals a problem and means it's time to call the vet.

A dog's ears should be cleaned regularly; once a week is suggested, and you can do this along with your regular brushing. Using a cotton ball or pad, and never probing into the ear canal, wipe the ear gently. You can use an ear-cleansing liquid or powder available from your vet or pet-supply store; alternatively, you might prefer to use home-made solutions with ingredients like one part white vinegar and one part hydrogen peroxide. Ask your vet about home remedies before you attempt to concoct something on your own!

Keep your dog's ears free of excess hair by carefully cutting it as needed. If done gently, this will be painless for the dog. Look for wax, brown droppings (a sign of ear mites), redness or any other abnormalities. At the first sign of a problem, contact your vet so that he can prescribe an appropriate medication.

Eye Care

During grooming sessions, pay extra attention to the condition of your dog's eyes. If the area around the eyes is soiled or if tear staining has occurred, there are various cleaning agents made especially for this purpose. Look at the dog's eyes to make sure no debris has entered; dogs with large eyes and those who spend time outdoors are especially prone to this.

The signs of an eye infection are obvious: mucus, redness, puffiness, scabs or other signs of irritation. If your dog's eyes become infected, the vet will likely prescribe an antibiotic ointment for treatment. If you notice signs of more serious problems, such as opacities in the eye, which usually indicate cataracts, consult the vet at once. Taking time to pay attention to your dog's eyes will alert you in the early stages of any problem so that you can get your dog treatment as soon as possible. You could save your dog's sight!

A Clean Smile

Another essential part of grooming is brushing your dog's teeth and checking his overall oral condition. Studies show that around 80% of dogs experience dental problems by two years of age, and the percentage is higher in older dogs. Therefore it is highly likely that your dog will have trouble with his teeth and gums unless you are proactive with home dental care.

The most common dental problem in dogs is plaque build-up. If not treated, this causes gum disease, infection and resultant tooth loss. Bacteria from these infections spread throughout the body, affecting the vital organs. Do you need much more convincing to start brushing your dog's teeth? If so, take a good whiff of your dog's breath, and read on.

Fortunately, home dental care is rather easy and convenient for pet owners. Specially formulated canine toothpaste is easy to find. You should use one of these toothpastes, not a product for humans. Some doggie pastes are even available in flavors appealing to dogs. If your dog likes the flavor, he will tolerate the process better, making things much easier for you! Doggie toothbrushes come in different sizes and are designed to fit the contour of a canine mouth. Rubber fingertip brushes fit right on one of your fingers and have rubber nodes to clean the teeth and massage the gums. This may be easier to handle, as it is akin to rubbing your dog's teeth with your finger.

As with other grooming tasks, accustom your Clumber Spaniel pup to his dental care early on. Start gently, for a few minutes at a time, so that he gets used to the feel of the brush and to your handling his mouth. Offer praise and petting so that he looks at tooth-care time as a time when he gets extra love and attention. The routine should become second nature; he may not like it, but he should at least tolerate it.

Aside from brushing, offer dental toys to your dog and feed crunchy biscuits, which help to minimize plaque. Rope toys have the added benefit of acting like floss as the dog chews. At your adult dog's yearly check-ups, the vet will perform a a complete dental check for any problems and possibly a tooth-scraping. Proper care of your dog's teeth will ensure that you will enjoy your dog's smile for many years to come. The next time your dog goes to give you a hello kiss, you'll be glad you spent the time caring for his teeth.

The Other End

Dogs sometime have troubles with their anal glands, which are sacs located beside the anal vent. These should empty when a dog has normal bowel movements; if they don't, they can become full or impacted, causing discomfort. Owners often are alarmed to see their dogs scooting across the floor, dragging their behinds behind; this is just a dog's attempt to empty the glands himself.

Some brave owners attempt to evacuate their dogs' anal glands themselves during grooming, but no one will tell you that this is a pleasant task! Thus, many owners prefer to make the trip to the vet to have the vet take care of the problem; owners whose dogs visit a groomer can have this done by the groomer if he offers this as part of his services. Regardless, don't neglect the dog's other end in your home-care routine. Look for scooting, licking or other signs of discomfort "back there" to ascertain whether the anal glands need to be emptied.

ID FOR YOUR DOG

You love your Clumber Spaniel and want to keep him safe. Of course you take every precaution to prevent his escaping from the yard or becoming lost or stolen. You have a sturdy high fence and you always keep your dog on lead when out and about in public places. If your dog is not properly identified, however, you are overlooking a major aspect of his safety. We hope to never be in a situation where our dog is missing, but we should practice prevention in the unfortunate case that this happens; identification greatly increases the chances of your dog's being returned to you.

There are several ways to identify your dog. First, the

PET OR STRAY?

Besides the obvious benefit of providing your contact information to whoever finds your lost dog, an ID tag makes your dog more approachable and more likely to be recovered. A strange dog wandering the neighborhood without a collar and tags will look like a stray, while the collar and tags indicate that the dog is someone's pet. Even if the ID tags become detached from the collar, the collar alone will make a person more likely to pick up the dog.

traditional dog tag should be a staple in your dog's wardrobe, attached to his everyday collar. Tags can be made of sturdy plastic and various metals and should include your contact information so that a person who finds the dog can get in touch with you right away to arrange his return. Many people today enjoy the wide range of decorative tags available, so have fun and create a tag to match your dog's personality. Of course, it is important that the tag stays on the collar, so have a secure "O" ring attachment; you also can explore the type of tag that slides right onto the collar.

In addition to the ID tag, which every dog should wear even if identified by another method, two other forms of identification have become popular: microchipping and tattooing. In microchipping, a tiny scannable chip is painlessly inserted under the dog's skin. The number is registered to you so that, if your lost dog turns up at a clinic or shelter, the chip can be scanned to retrieve your contact information.

The advantage of the microchip is that it is a permanent form of ID, but there are some factors to consider. Several different companies make microchips, and not all are compatible with the others' scanning devices. It's best to find a company with a universal microchip that can be read by scanners made by other companies as well. It won't do any good to have the dog chipped if the information cannot be retrieved. Also, not every humane society,

Dogs should not be allowed to roam loose within a moving vehicle. Crate training pays off for traveling as well as housebreaking, as a crate keeps dogs safely confined while on the road.

shelter and clinic is equipped with a scanner, although more and more facilities are equipping themselves. In fact, many shelters microchip dogs that they adopt out to new homes.

Because the microchip is not visible to the eye, the dog must wear a tag that states that he is microchipped so that whoever picks him up will know to have him scanned. This tag usually also lists the registry's phone number and the dog's microchip ID number. He of course also should have a tag with your contact information in case his chip information cannot be retrieved. Humane societies and veterinary clinics offer microchipping service, which is usually very affordable.

Though less popular than microchipping, tattooing is another permanent method of ID for dogs. Most vets perform this service, and there are also clinics that perform dog tattooing. This is also an affordable procedure and one that will not cause much discomfort for the dog. It is best to put the tattoo in a visible area, such as the inside of an ear or the inside of a rear leg, to deter theft, although the tattoo may fade as the dog grows and be hard to locate. It is sad to say that there are cases of dogs' being stolen and sold to research laboratories, but such laboratories will not accept tattooed dogs.

To ensure that the tattoo is effective in aiding your dog's return to you, the tattoo number must be registered with a national organization. That way, when someone finds a tattooed dog, a phone call to the registry will quickly match the dog with his owner.

CAR CAUTION

You may like to bring your canine companion along on the daily errands, but if you will be running in and out from place to place and can't bring him indoors with you, leave him at home. Your dog should never be left alone in the car, not even for a minute—never! A car heats up very quickly, and even a cracked-open window will not help. In fact, leaving the window cracked will be dangerous if the dog becomes uncomfortable and tries to escape. A dog left alone in a car can also be a target for thieves. When in doubt, leave your dog home, where you know he will be safe.

If your breeder lives a reasonable distance from your home, boarding your Clumber with his breeder may be a viable option while you are on vacation.

TRAINING YOUR

CLUMBER SPANIEL

BASIC TRAINING PRINCIPLES: PUPPY VS. ADULT

There's a big difference between training an adult dog and training a young puppy. With a young puppy, everything is new. When your Clumber pup first comes home with you, he will be experiencing many things, and he has nothing with which to compare these experiences. Up to this point, he has been with his dam and littermates, not one-on-one with people except in his interactions with his breeder and visitors to the litter.

When you first bring the puppy home, he is eager to please you. This means that he accepts doing things your way. During the next couple of months, he will absorb the basis of everything he needs to know for the rest of his life. This early age is even referred to as the "sponge" stage. After that, for the next 18 months, it's up to you to reinforce good manners by building on the foundation that you've established. Once your puppy is reliable in basic commands and behavior and has reached the appropriate age, you may gradually introduce him to some of the interesting sports, games and activities available to pet owners and their dogs.

Raising your puppy is a family affair. Each member of the family must know what rules to set forth for the puppy and how to use the same one-word commands to mean exactly the same thing every time. Even if yours is a large family, one person will soon be considered by the pup to be the leader, the alpha person in his pack, the "boss" who must be obeyed. Often that highly regarded person turns out to be the one who feeds the puppy. Food ranks very high on the puppy's list of important things. That's why your puppy is rewarded with small treats along with verbal praise when he responds to you correctly. As the puppy learns to do what you want him to do, the food rewards are gradually eliminated and only the praise remains. If you were to keep up with the food treats, you could have two problems on your hands—an obese dog and a beggar.

Training begins the minute

The Clumber Spaniel loves children and is happy to get a glimpse of the world through the eyes of a young friend.

your Clumber Spaniel puppy steps through the doorway of your home, so don't make the mistake of putting the puppy on the floor and telling him by your actions to "Go for it! Run wild!" Even if this is your first puppy, you must act as if you know what you're doing: be the boss. An uncertain pup may be terrified to move, while a bold one will be ready to take you at your word and start plotting to destroy the house! Before you collected your puppy, you decided where his own special place would be, and that's where to put him when you first arrive home. Give him a house tour after he has investigated his area and had a nap and a bathroom "pit stop."

It's worth mentioning here that if you've adopted an adult dog that is completely trained to your liking, lucky you! You're off the hook! However, if that dog spent his life up to this point in a kennel, or even in a good home but without any real training, be prepared to tackle the job ahead. An adult dog with no previous training cannot be blamed for not knowing what he was never taught. While the dog is trying to understand and learn your rules, at the same time he has to unlearn many of his previously self-taught habits and general view of the world.

Working with a professional trainer will speed up your progress with an adopted adult dog. You'll need patience, too. Some new rules may be close to

SMILE WHEN YOU ORDER ME AROUND!

While trainers recommend practicing with your dog every day, it's perfectly acceptable to take a "mental health day" off. It's better not to train the dog on days when you're in a sour mood. Your bad attitude or lack of interest will be sensed by your dog, and he will respond accordingly. Studies show that dogs are well tuned in to their humans' emotions. Be conscious of how you use your voice when talking to your dog. Raising your voice or shouting will only erode your dog's trust in you as his trainer and master.

impossible for the dog to accept. After all, he's been successful so far by doing everything his way! (Patience again.) He may agree with your instruction for a few days and then slip back into his old ways, so you must be just as consistent and understanding in your teaching as you would be with a puppy. (More patience needed yet again!) Your dog has to learn to pay attention to your voice, your family, the daily routine, new smells, new sounds and, in some cases, even a new climate.

One of the most important things to find out about a newly adopted adult dog is his reaction to children (yours and others), strangers and your friends, and how he acts upon meeting other dogs. If he was not socialized with dogs as a puppy, this could be a major problem. This does not mean that he's a "bad" dog, a vicious dog or an aggressive dog; rather, it means that he has no idea how to read another dog's body language. There's no way for him to tell whether the other dog is a friend or foe. Survival instinct takes over, telling him to attack first and ask questions later. This definitely calls for professional help and, even then, may not be a behavior that can be corrected 100% reliably (or even at all). If you have a puppy, this is why it is so very important to introduce your young puppy properly to other puppies and "dog-friendly" adult dogs. Behavior problems due to lack of training or lack of socialization can be avoided by communication with your dog and time committed to his proper training and upbringing.

OUR CANINE KIDS

"Everything I learned about parenting, I learned from my dog." How often adults recognize that their parenting skills are mere extensions of the education they acquired while caring for their dogs. Many owners refer to their dogs as their "kids" and treat their canine companions like real members of the family. Surveys indicate that a majority of dog owners talk to their dogs regularly, celebrate their dogs' birthdays and purchase Christmas gifts for their dogs. Another survey shows that dog owners take their dogs to the veterinarian more frequently than they visit their own physicians.

Clumbers love children and are very patient with young friends. This child is having no luck lead-training her tolerant Clumber chum.

HOUSE-TRAINING YOUR CLUMBER SPANIEL

Dogs are tactility-oriented when it comes to house-training. In other words, they respond to the surface on which they are given approval to eliminate. The choice is yours (the dog's version is in parentheses): The lawn (including the neighbors' lawns)? A bare patch of earth under a tree (where people like to sit and relax in the summertime)? Concrete steps or patio (all sidewalks, garages and basement floors)? The curbside (watch out for cars)? A small area of crushed stone in a corner of the yard (mine!)? The latter is the best choice if you can manage it, because it will remain strictly for the dog's use and is easy to keep clean.

You can start out with paper-training indoors and switch over to an outdoor surface as the puppy matures and gains control over his need to eliminate. For the nay-sayers, don't worry—this won't mean that the dog will soil on every piece of newspaper lying around the house. You are training him to go outside, remember? Starting out by paper-training often is the only choice for a city dog.

When Your Puppy's "Got to Go"

Your puppy's need to relieve himself is seemingly non-stop, but signs of improvement will be seen each week. While you do not need to begin teaching basic commands immediately, you do need to start house-training as soon as puppy comes home. From 8–10 weeks old, the puppy will have to be taken outside every time he wakes up, about 10–15 minutes after every meal and after every period of play—all day long, from first thing in the morning until his bedtime! That's a total of ten or more trips per day to teach the puppy where it's okay to relieve himself. With that schedule in mind, you can see that house-training a young puppy is not a part-time job. It requires someone to be home all day.

If that seems overwhelming or impossible, do a little planning. For example, plan to pick up your puppy at the start of a vacation period. If you can't get home in the middle of the day, plan to hire a dog-sitter or ask a neighbor to come over to take the pup outside, feed him his lunch and then take him out again about ten or so minutes after he's eaten. Also make arrangements with that or another person to be your "emergency" contact if you have to stay late on the job. Remind yourself—repeatedly—that this hectic schedule improves as the puppy gets older.

Home within a Home

Your Clumber Spaniel puppy needs to be confined to one secure, puppy-proof area when no one is able to watch his every move. Generally the kitchen is the place of choice because the floor is washable. Likewise, it's a busy family area that will accustom the pup to a variety of noises, everything from pots and pans to the telephone, blender and dishwasher. He will also be enchanted by the smell of your cooking (and will never be critical when you burn something). A sturdy exercise pen (also called an "ex-pen," a puppy version of a playpen), with high enough sides to contain the puppy, within the room of choice can be a good means of confinement for a young pup. He can see out and has a certain amount of space in which to run about, but he is safe from dangerous things like electrical cords, heating units,

A Clumber and friends are a captive audience for the snacktime performance.

POTTY COMMAND

Most dogs love to please their masters; there are no bounds to what dogs will do to make their owners happy. The potty command is a good example of this theory. If toileting on command makes the master happy, then more power to him. Puppies will obligingly piddle if it really makes their keepers smile. Some owners can be creative about which word they will use to command their dogs to relieve themselves. Some popular choices are "Potty," "Tinkle," "Piddle," "Let's go," "Hurry up" and "Toilet." Give the command every time your puppy goes into position and the puppy will begin to associate his business with the command.

Canine Development Schedule

It is important to understand how and at what age a puppy develops into adulthood. If you are a puppy owner, consult this Canine Development Schedule to determine the stage of development your puppy is currently experiencing. This knowledge will help you as you work with the puppy in the weeks and months ahead.

Period	Age	Characteristics
First to Third	Birth to Seven Weeks	Puppy needs food, sleep and warmth and responds to simple and gentle touching. Needs mother for security and disciplining. Needs littermates for learning and interacting with other dogs. Pup learns to function within a pack and learns pack order of dominance. Begin socializing pup with adults and children for short periods. Pup begins to become aware of his environment.
Fourth	Eight to Twelve Weeks	Brain is fully developed. Pup needs socializing with outside world. Remove from mother and littermates. Needs to change from canine pack to human pack. Human dominance necessary. Fear period occurs between 8 and 12 weeks. Avoid fright and pain.
Fifth	Thirteen to Sixteen Weeks	Training and formal obedience should begin. Less association with other dogs, more with people, places, situations. Period will pass easily if you remember this is pup's change-to-adolescence time. Be firm and fair. Flight instinct prominent. Permissiveness and over-disciplining can do permanent damage. Praise for good behavior.
Juvenile	Four to Eight Months	Another fear period about seven to eight months of age. It passes quickly, but be cautious of fright and pain. Sexual maturity reached. Dominant traits established. Dog should understand sit, down, come and stay by now.

Note: These are approximate time frames. Allow for individual differences in puppies.

trash baskets or open kitchen-supply cabinets. Place the pen where the puppy will not get a blast of heat or air conditioning.

In the pen, you can put a few long-lasting toys, his bed (which can be his crate if the dimensions of pen and crate are compatible) and a few layers of newspaper in one small corner, just in case. A water bowl can be hung at a convenient height on the side of the ex-pen so it won't become a splashing pool for an innovative puppy. His food dish can go on the floor, but not under the water bowl.

Crates are something that pet owners are at last getting used to for their dogs. Wild or domestic canines have always preferred to sleep in den-like safe spots, and that is exactly what the crate provides. How often have you seen adult dogs that choose to sleep under a table or chair even though they have full run of the house? It's the den connection.

In your "happy" voice, use the word "Crate" every time you put the pup into his den. If he's new to a crate, toss in a small biscuit for him to chase the first few times. At night, after he's been outside, he should sleep in his crate. The crate may be kept in his designated area at night or, if you want to be sure to hear those wake-up yips in the morning, put the crate in a corner of your bedroom. However, don't

Carrying your puppy to his potty spot is not recommended. Lead him there on his leash; potty training and leash training go hand in hand.

TIDY BOY

Clean by nature, dogs do not like to soil their dens, which in effect are their crates or sleeping quarters. Unless not feeling well, dogs will not defecate or urinate in their crates. Crate training capitalizes on the dog's natural desire to keep his den clean. Be conscientious about giving the puppy as many opportunities to relieve himself outdoors as possible. Reward the puppy for correct behavior. Praise him and pat him whenever he "goes" in the correct location. Even the tidiest of puppies can have potty accidents, so be patient and dedicate more energy to helping your puppy achieve a clean lifestyle.

make any response whatsoever to whining or crying. If he's completely ignored, he'll settle down and get to sleep.

Good bedding for a young puppy is an old folded bath towel or an old blanket, something that is easily washable and disposable if necessary ("accidents" will happen!). Never put newspaper in the puppy's crate. Also, those old ideas about adding a clock to replace his mother's heartbeat, or a hot-water bottle to replace her warmth, are just that—old ideas. The clock could drive the puppy nuts, and the hot-water bottle could end up as a very soggy waterbed! An extremely good breeder would have introduced your puppy to the crate by letting two pups sleep together for a couple of nights, followed by several nights alone. How thankful you will be if you found that breeder!

Safe toys in the pup's crate or area will keep him occupied, but monitor their condition closely. Discard any toys that show signs of being chewed to bits. Squeaky parts, bits of stuffing or plastic or any other small pieces can cause intestinal blockage or possibly choking if swallowed.

Also remember that dogs get bored. It is not fair to leave a dog in a crate because it is convenient for you to put him away. He should be left in his crate for as short a time as possible, except overnight. You may find that as the dog grows up, he will go into his crate on his own and enjoy napping with the door open.

LEASH TRAINING

House-training and leash training go hand in hand, literally. When taking your puppy outside to do his business, lead him there on his leash. Unless an emergency potty run is called for, do not whisk the puppy up into your arms and take him outside. If you have a fenced yard, you have the advantage of letting the puppy loose to go out, but it's better to put the dog on the leash and take him to his designated place in the yard until he is reliably house-trained. Taking the puppy for a walk is the best way to house-train a dog. The dog will associate the walk with his time to relieve himself, and the exercise of walking stimulates the dog's bowels and bladder. Dogs that are not trained to relieve themselves on a walk may hold it until they get back home, which of course defeats half the purpose of the walk.

Progressing with Potty-Training

After you've taken your puppy out and he has relieved himself in the area you've selected, he can have some free time with the family as long as there is someone responsible for watching him. That doesn't mean just someone in the same room who is watching TV or busy on the computer, but one person who is doing nothing other than keeping an eye on the pup, playing with him on the floor and helping him understand his position in the pack.

This first taste of freedom will let you begin to set the house rules. If you don't want the dog on the furniture, now is the time to prevent his first attempts to jump up onto the couch. The word to use in this case is "Off," not "Down." "Down" is the word you will use to teach the down position, which is something entirely different.

Most corrections at this stage come in the form of simply distracting the puppy. Instead of telling him "No" for "Don't chew the carpet," distract the chomping puppy with a toy and he'll forget about the carpet.

A family portrait. From left to right: Tessa, Klondike, mom Crystal, Beau and Brit.

As you are playing with the pup, do not forget to watch him closely and pay attention to his body language. Whenever you see him begin to circle or sniff, take the puppy outside to relieve himself. If you are paper-training, put him back into his confined area on the newspapers. In either case, praise him as he eliminates while he actually is in the act of relieving himself. Three seconds after he has finished is too late! You'll be praising him for running toward you, picking up a toy or whatever he may be doing at that moment, and that's not what you want to be praising him for. Timing is a vital tool in all dog training. Use it.

Remove soiled newspapers immediately and replace them with clean ones. You may want to take a small piece of soiled paper and place it in the middle of the new clean papers, as the scent will attract him to that spot when it's time to go again. That

DAILY SCHEDULE

How many relief trips does your puppy need per day? A puppy up to the age of 14 weeks will need to go outside about 8 to 12 times per day! You will have to take the pup out any time he starts sniffing around the floor or turning in small circles, as well as after naps, meals, games and lessons or whenever he's released from his crate. Once the puppy is 14 to 22 weeks of age, he will require only 6 to 8 relief trips. At the ages of 22 to 32 weeks, the puppy will require about 5 to 7 trips. Adult dogs typically require 4 relief trips per day, in the morning, afternoon, evening and late at night.

SOMEBODY TO BLAME

A puppy does not instinctively understand the difference between defecating on the pavement outside and on the kitchen floor. He is confused and frightened by his human's exuberant reactions to his natural urges. The owner, arguably the more intelligent of the duo, can get frustrated that he cannot convince his puppy to obey his commands and instructions. However, harsh corrections are inappropriate during house-training. Don't blame the puppy, blame yourself for not being 100% consistent with the routine. Be patient and diligent, and puppy will succeed.

scent attraction is why it's so important to clean up any messes made in the house by using a product specially made to eliminate the odor of dog urine and droppings. Regular household cleansers won't do the trick. Pet shops sell the best pet deodorizers. Invest in the largest container you can find.

Scent attraction eventually will lead your pup to his chosen spot outdoors; this is the basis of outdoor training. When you take your puppy outside to relieve himself, use a one-word command such as "Outside" or "Go-potty" (that's one word to the puppy!) as you attach his leash. Then lead him to his spot. Now comes the hard part—hard for you, that is. Just stand there until he urinates and defecates. Move him a few feet in one direction or another if he's just sitting there looking at you, but remember that this is neither playtime nor time for a walk. This is strictly a business trip. Then, as he circles and squats (remember your timing!), give him a quiet "Good dog" as praise. If you start to jump for joy, ecstatic over his performance, he'll do one of two things: either he will stop mid-stream, as it were, or he'll do it again for you—in the house—and expect you to be just as delighted.

Give him five minutes or so and, if he doesn't go in that time, take him back indoors to his confined area and try again in another ten minutes, or immediately if you see him sniffing and circling. By careful observation, you'll soon work out a successful schedule.

Accidents, by the way, are just that—accidents. Clean them up quickly and thoroughly, without comment, after the puppy has been taken outside to finish his business and then put back into his area or crate. If you witness an accident in progress, say "No!" in a stern voice and get the pup outdoors immediately. No punishment is needed. You and your puppy are just learning each other's language, and sometimes it's easy to miss a puppy's message. Chalk it up to experience and watch more closely from now on.

KEEPING THE PACK ORDERLY

Discipline is a form of training that brings order to life. For example, military discipline is what allows the soldiers in an army to work as one. Discipline is a form of teaching and, in dogs, is the basis of how the successful pack operates. Each member knows his place in the pack and all respect the leader, or alpha dog. It is essential for your puppy that you establish this type of relationship, with you as the alpha, or leader. It is a form of social coexistence that all canines recognize and accept. Discipline, therefore, is never to be confused with punishment. When you teach your puppy how you want him to behave, and he behaves properly and you praise him for it, you are disciplining him with a form of positive reinforcement.

TONE OF VOICE

Most trainers suggest that an owner never use "baby talk" with the dog. However, the tone of voice used in connection with that type of "language" is almost always responded to in a positive way by any dog. Baby talk can be used at home for fun, but never should be used in training.

Keeping order within the pack demands that your Clumber be discouraged at an early age from begging while food—his or yours—is being prepared.

For a dog, rewards come in the form of praise, a smile, a cheerful tone of voice, a few friendly pats or a rub of the ears. Rewards are also small food treats. Obviously, that does not mean bits of regular dog food. Instead, treats are very small bits of special things like cheese or pieces of soft dog treats. The idea is to reward the dog with something very small that he can taste and swallow, providing instant positive reinforcement. If he has to take time to chew the treat, by the time he is finished he will have forgotten what he did to earn it!

Your puppy should never be

Food...the universal language! When used properly, treats work wonders to keep a dog focused and motivated during training.

physically punished. The displeasure shown on your face and in your voice is sufficient to signal to the pup that he has done something wrong. He wants to please everyone higher up on the social ladder, especially his leader, so a scowl and harsh voice will take care of the error. Growling out the word "Shame!" when the pup is caught in the act of doing something wrong is better than the repetitive "No." Some dogs hear "No" so often that they begin to think it's their name! By the way, do not use the dog's name when you're correcting him. His name is reserved to get his attention for something pleasant about to take place.

There are punishments that have nothing to do with you. For example, your dog may think that chasing cats is one reason for his existence. You can try to stop it as much as you like but without success, because it's such fun for the dog. But one good hissing, spitting swipe of a cat's claws across the dog's nose will put an end to the game forever. Intervene only when your dog's eyeball is seriously at risk. Cat scratches can cause permanent damage to an innocent but annoying puppy.

PUPPY KINDERGARTEN

Collar and Leash

Before you begin your Clumber Spaniel puppy's education, he must be used to his collar and leash. Choose a collar for your puppy that is secure, but not heavy or bulky. He won't enjoy training if he's uncomfortable. Most Clumber owners use a soft nylon slip collar. A chain choke collar wears away the dog's neck hair, and pinch or prong collars are never necessary for a Clumber Spaniel. Remember to check the size of the collar as the dog grows so that it is not too tight.

A 6-foot lead is used for training and can be used to walk your dog, but a retractable lead is best for simply exercising your dog. Never use a chain lead as it is too heavy and not necessary for this breed.

If you've been wise enough to enroll in a puppy kindergarten training class, suggestions will be made as to the best collar and leash for your young puppy. I say "wise" because your puppy will be in a class with puppies in his age range (up to five months old) of all breeds and sizes. It's the perfect way for him to learn the right way (and the wrong way) to interact with other dogs as well as their people. You cannot teach your puppy how to interpret another dog's sign language. For a first-time puppy owner, these socialization classes are invaluable. For experienced dog owners, they are a real boon to further training.

Attention

You've been using the dog's name since the minute you collected him from the breeder, so you should be able to get his attention by saying his name—with a big smile and in an excited tone of voice. His response will be the puppy equivalent of "Here I am! What are we going to do?" Your immediate response (if you haven't guessed by now) is "Good dog." Rewarding him at the moment he pays attention to you teaches him the proper way to respond when he hears his name.

"OK, what's next?" This happy and attentive Clumber is ready for his owner's instructions.

EXERCISES FOR A BASIC CANINE EDUCATION

The Sit Exercise

There are several ways to teach the puppy to sit. The first one is to catch him whenever he is about to sit and, as his backside nears the floor, say "Sit, good dog!" That's positive reinforcement and, if your timing is sharp, he will learn that what he's doing at that second is connected to your saying "Sit" and that you think he's clever for doing it!

Another method is to start with the puppy on his leash in front of you. Show him a treat in the palm of your right hand. Bring your hand up under his nose and, almost in slow motion, move your hand up and back so his nose goes up in the air and his head tilts back as he follows the treat in your hand. At that point, he will have to either sit or fall over, so as his back legs buckle under, say "Sit, good dog," and then give him the treat and lots of praise. You may have to begin with your hand lightly running up his chest, actually lifting his chin up until he sits. Some (usually older) dogs require gentle pressure on their hindquarters with the left hand, in which case the dog should be on your left side. Puppies generally do not appreciate this physical dominance.

After a few times, you should be able to show the dog a treat in the open palm of your hand, raise your hand waist-high as you say "Sit" and have him sit. You thereby will have taught him two things at the same time. Both the verbal command and the motion of the hand are signals for the sit. Your puppy is watching you almost more than he is listening to you, so what you do is just as

A SIMPLE "SIT"

When you command your dog to sit, use the word "Sit." Do not say "Sit down," as your dog will not know whether you mean "Sit" or "Down," or maybe you mean both. Be clear in your instructions to your dog; use one-word commands and always be consistent.

important as what you say.

Don't save any of these drills only for training sessions. Use them as much as possible at odd times during a normal day. The dog should always sit before being given his food dish. He should sit to let you go through a doorway first, when the doorbell rings or when you stop to speak to someone on the street.

The Down Exercise

Before beginning to teach the down command, you must consider how the dog feels about this exercise. To him, "down" is a submissive position. Being flat on the floor with you standing over him is not his idea of fun. It's up to you to let him know that, while it may not be fun, the reward of your approval is worth his effort.

Start with the puppy on your left side in a sit position. Hold the leash right above his collar in your left hand. Have an extra-special treat, such as a small piece of cooked chicken or hot dog, in your right hand. Place it at the end of the pup's nose and steadily move your hand down and forward along the ground. Hold the leash to prevent a sudden lunge for the food. As the puppy goes into the down position, say "Down" very gently.

The difficulty with this exercise is twofold: it's both the submissive aspect and the fact that most people say the word "Down" as if they were drill sergeants in charge of recruits! So issue the command sweetly, give him the treat and have the pup maintain the down position for several seconds. If he tries to get up immediately, place your hands on his shoulders and press down gently, giving him a very quiet

Clumbers can be stubborn in learning the down exercise. Never intimidate a dog to teach him this (or any) command, as forceful methods will yield no results with a Clumber.

DOWN

"Down" is a harsh-sounding word and a submissive posture in dog body language, thus presenting two obstacles in teaching the down command. When the dog is about to flop down on his own, tell him "Good down." Pups that are not good about being handled learn better by having food lowered in front of them. A dog that trusts you can be gently guided into position. When you give the command "Down," be sure to say it sweetly!

"Good dog." As you progress with this lesson, increase the "down time" until he will hold it until you say "Okay" (his cue for release). Practice this one in the house at various times throughout the day.

By increasing the length of time during which the dog must maintain the down position, you'll find many uses for it. For example, he can lie at your feet in the vet's office or anywhere that both of you have to wait, when you are on the phone, while the family is eating and so forth. If you progress to training for competitive obedience, he'll already be all set for the exercise called the "long down."

WHO'S TRAINING WHOM?

Dog training is a black-and-white exercise. The correct response to a command must be absolute, and the trainer must insist on completely accurate responses from the dog. A trainer cannot command his dog to sit and then settle for the dog's melting into the down position. Often owners are so pleased that their dogs "did something" in response to a command that they just shrug and say, "OK, down" even though they wanted the dog to sit. You want your dog to respond to the command without hesitation: he must respond at that moment and correctly every time.

Keeping training sessions fun, with plenty of hugs, will convince your Clumber that training time is something to look forward to.

The Stay Exercise

You can teach your Clumber Spaniel to stay in the sit, down and stand positions. To teach the sit/stay, have the dog sit on your left side. Hold the leash at waist level in your left hand and let the dog know that you have a treat in your closed right hand. Step forward on your right foot as you say "Stay." Immediately turn and stand directly in front of the dog, keeping your right hand up high so he'll keep his eye on the treat hand and maintain the sit position for a count of five. Return to your original position and offer the reward.

Increase the length of the sit/stay each time until the dog can hold it for at least 30 seconds without moving. After about a week of success, move out on your right foot and take two steps before turning to face the dog. Give the "Stay" hand signal (left palm held up, facing the dog) as you leave. He gets the treat when you return and he holds the sit/stay. Increase the distance that you walk away from him before turning until you reach the length of your training leash. But don't rush it! Go back to the beginning if he moves before he should. No matter what the lesson, never be upset by having to back up for a few days. The repetition and practice are what will make your dog reliable in these commands. It won't do any good to move on to something more difficult if the command is not mastered at the easier levels. Above all, even if you do get frustrated, never let your puppy know. Always keep a positive, upbeat attitude during training, which will transmit to your dog for positive results.

The down/stay is taught in the same way once the dog is completely reliable and steady with the down command. Again, don't rush it. With the dog in the down position on your left side, step out on your right foot as you say "Stay." Return by walking around in back of the dog and into your original position. While you are training, it's okay to murmur something like "Hold on" to encourage him to stay put. When the dog will stay without moving when you are at a distance of 3 or 4 feet, begin to increase the length of time before you return. Be sure he holds the down on your return until you

Teach the sit/stay with the dog in a sit position on your left side before stepping out in front of him. Use hand signals to reinforce your commands.

Be firm with your Clumber, but never harsh or unkind. A simple word of scolding is usually enough to get the point across.

Most Clumbers have a favorite toy, which can be used to entice him to come to you or to invite him to play.

say "Okay." At that point, he gets his treat—just so he'll remember for next time that it's not over until it's over.

The Come Exercise

No command is more important to the safety of your Clumber Spaniel than "Come." It is what you should say every single time you see the puppy running toward you: "Charlie, come! Good dog." During playtime, run a few feet away from the puppy and turn and tell him to "Come" as he is already running to you. You can go so far as to teach your puppy two things at once if you squat down and hold out your arms. As the pup gets close to you and you're saying "Good dog," bring your right arm in about waist high. Now he's also learning the hand signal, an excellent device should you be on the phone when you need to get him to come to you! You'll also both be one step ahead when you enter obedience classes.

When the puppy responds to your well-timed "Come," try it with the puppy on the training leash. This time, catch him off guard, while he's sniffing a leaf or watching a bird: "Charlie, come!" You may have to pause for a split second after his name to be sure you have his attention. If the puppy shows any sign of confusion, give the leash a mild jerk and take a couple of steps backward. Do not repeat the command. In this case, you should say

TIPS FOR TRAINING AND SAFETY

1. Whether on or off leash, practice only in a fenced area.
2. Remove the training collar when the training session is over.
3. Don't try to break up a dogfight.
4. "Come," "Leave it" and "Wait" are safety commands.
5. The dog belongs in a crate or behind a barrier when riding in the car.
6. Don't ignore the dog's first sign of aggression. Aggression only gets worse, so take it seriously.
7. Keep the faces of children and dogs separated.
8. Pay attention to what the dog is chewing.
9. Keep the vet's number near your phone.
10. "Okay" is a useful release command.

"Good come" as he reaches you.

That's the number-one rule of training. Each command word is given just once. Anything more is nagging. You'll also notice that all commands are one word only. Even when they are actually two words, you say them as one.

Never call the dog to come to you—with or without his name—if you are angry or intend to correct him for some misbehavior. When correcting the pup, you go to him. Your dog must always connect "Come" with something pleasant and with your approval; then you can rely on his response.

Puppies, like children, have notoriously short attention spans, so don't overdo it with any of the training. Keep each lesson short. Break it up with a quick run around the yard or a ball toss, repeat the lesson and quit as soon as the pup gets it right. That way, you will always end with a "Good dog."

Life isn't perfect and neither are puppies. A time will come, often around ten months of age, when he'll become "selectively deaf" or choose to "forget" his name. He may respond by wagging his tail (and even seeming to smile at you) with a look that says "Make me!" Laugh, throw his favorite toy and skip the lesson you had planned. Pups will be pups!

The Heel Exercise

The second most important command to teach, after the

Daily walks can be pleasurable or a struggle, depending on your Clumber's on-leash behavior.

A properly heeling Clumber is a joy to walk with from all angles.

come, is the heel. When you are walking your growing puppy, you need to be in control. Besides, it looks terrible to be pulled and yanked down the street, and it's not much fun either. Your puppy will probably follow you everywhere when he first comes home, but that's his natural instinct, not your control over the situation. However, any time he does follow you, you can say "Heel" and be ahead of the game, as he will learn to associate this command with the action of following you before you even begin teaching him to heel.

There is a very precise, almost military, procedure for teaching your dog to heel. As with all other obedience training, begin with the dog on your left side. He will be in a very nice sit and you will have the training leash across your chest. Hold the loop and folded leash in your right hand. Pick up the slack leash above the dog in your left hand and hold it loosely at your side. Step out on your left foot as you say "Heel." If the puppy does not move, give a gentle tug or pat your left leg to get him started. If he surges ahead of you, stop and pull him back gently until he is at your side. Tell him to sit and begin again.

Walk a few steps and stop while the puppy is correctly beside you. Tell him to sit and give mild verbal praise. (More

MORE PRAISE, LESS FOOD

As you progress with your puppy's lessons, and the puppy is responding well, gradually begin to wean him off the treats by alternating the treats with times when you offer only verbal praise or a few pats on the dog's side. (Pats on the head are dominant actions, so he won't think they are meant to be praise.) Every lesson should end with the puppy's performing the correct action for that session's command. When he gets it right and you withhold the treat, the praise can be as long and lavish as you like. The commands are one word only, but your verbal praise can use as many words as you want—don't skimp!

enthusiastic praise will encourage him to think the lesson is over.) Repeat the lesson, increasing the number of steps you take only as long as the dog is heeling nicely beside you. When you end the lesson, have him hold the sit, then give him the "Okay" to let him know that this is the end of the lesson. Praise him so that he knows he did a good job.

The cure for excessive pulling (a common problem) is to stop when the dog is no more than 2 or 3 feet ahead of you. Guide him back into position and begin again. With a really determined puller, try switching to a head collar. This will automatically turn the pup's head toward you so you can bring him back easily to the heel position. Give quiet, reassuring praise every time the leash goes slack and he's staying with you.

Staying and heeling can take a lot out of a dog, so provide playtime and free-running exercise to shake off the stress when the lessons are over. You don't want him to associate training with all work and no fun.

TAPERING OFF TIDBITS

Your dog has been watching you—and the hand that treats—throughout all of his lessons, and now it's time to break the treat habit. Begin by giving him treats at the end of each lesson only. Then start to give a treat after the end of only some of the lessons. At the end of every lesson, as well as during the lessons, be consistent with the praise. Your pup now doesn't know whether he'll get a treat or not, but he should keep performing well just in case! Finally, you will stop giving treat rewards entirely. Save them for something brand-new that you want to teach him. Keep up the praise and you'll always have a "good dog."

OBEDIENCE CLASSES

The advantages of an obedience class are that your dog will have to learn amid the distractions of

Who says that Clumbers are lazy?! Engage your Clumber in a vigorous game of fetch and he will come to life and play like a puppy.

other people and dogs and that your mistakes will be quickly corrected by the trainer. Teaching your dog along with a qualified instructor and other handlers who may have more dog experience than you is another plus of the class environment. The instructor and other handlers can help you to find the most efficient way of teaching your dog a command or exercise. It's often easier to learn from other people's mistakes than your own. You will also learn all of the requirements for competitive

Nearly flying over the A-frame, this Clumber Spaniel makes agility competition look easy.

BE UPSTANDING!
You are the dog's leader. During training, stand up straight so your dog looks up at you, and therefore up *to* you. Say the command words distinctly, in a clear, declarative tone of voice. (No barking!) Give rewards only as the correct response takes place (remember your timing!). Praise, smiles and treats are "rewards" used to positively reinforce correct responses. Don't repeat a mistake. Just change to another exercise—you will soon find success!

obedience trials, in which you can earn titles and go on to advanced jumping and retrieving exercises, which are fun for many dogs. Obedience classes build the foundation needed for many other canine activities (in which we humans are allowed to participate, too!).

TRAINING FOR OTHER ACTIVITIES

Once your dog has basic obedience under his collar and is 12 months of age, you can enter the world of agility training. Dogs think agility is pure fun, like being turned loose in an amusement park full of obstacles! In addition to agility, there are different types of competition geared toward certain breeds or groups of breeds. Clumber Spaniels and their owners may enjoy participating in hunting events, and Clumbers also enjoy tracking, which is open to all "nosey" dogs (which would include all dogs!). For those who like to volunteer, there is the wonderful feeling of owning a therapy dog and visiting hospices, nursing homes and veterans' homes to bring smiles, comfort and companionship to those who live there.

Around the house, your Clumber Spaniel can be taught to do some simple chores. You might teach him to carry some small household items or to fetch the morning newspaper. The kids can teach the dog all kinds of tricks, from playing hide-and-seek to balancing a biscuit on his nose. A family dog is what rounds out the family. Everything he does, including sitting at your feet and gazing lovingly at you, represents the bonus of owning a dog and bonds you to him.

Some spectators are surprised by the Clumber's aptitude on the agility course. This dog navigates the weave poles with speed and accuracy.

Physical Structure of the Clumber Spaniel

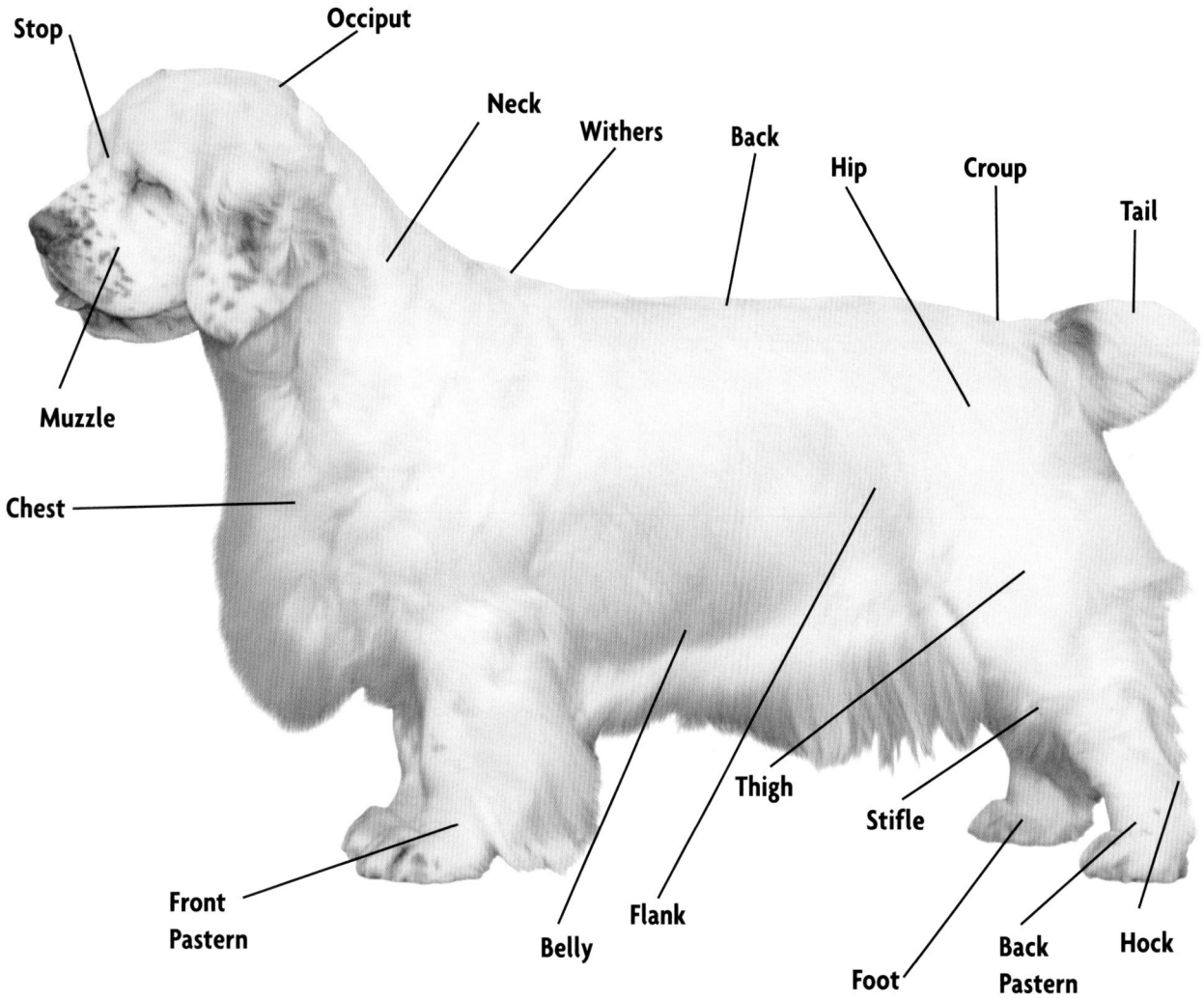

HEALTHCARE OF YOUR

CLUMBER SPANIEL

BY LOWELL ACKERMAN DVM, DACVD

HEALTHCARE FOR A LIFETIME

When you own a dog, you become his healthcare advocate over his entire lifespan, as well as being the one to shoulder the financial burden of such care. Accordingly, it is worthwhile to focus on prevention rather than treatment, as you and your pet will both be happier.

Of course, the best place to have begun your program of preventive healthcare is with the initial purchase or adoption of your dog. There is no way of guaranteeing that your new furry friend is free of medical problems, but there are some things you can do to improve your odds. You certainly should have done adequate research into the Clumber Spaniel and have selected your puppy carefully rather than buying on impulse. Health issues aside, a large number of pet abandonment and relinquishment cases arise from a mismatch between pet needs and owner expectations. This is entirely preventable with appropriate planning and finding a good breeder.

Regarding healthcare issues specifically, it is very difficult to make blanket statements about where to acquire a problem-free pet, but, again, a reputable breeder is your best bet. In an ideal situation you have the opportunity to see both parents, get references from other owners of the breeder's pups and see genetic-testing documentation for several generations of the litter's ancestors. At the very least, you must thoroughly investigate the Clumber Spaniel and the problems inherent in the breed, as well as the genetic testing

Dr. Roe Froman is a veterinarian who specializes in Clumber Spaniels. Here she is shown examining a four-week-old Clumber puppy to evaluate its general health.

Internal Organs of the Clumber Spaniel

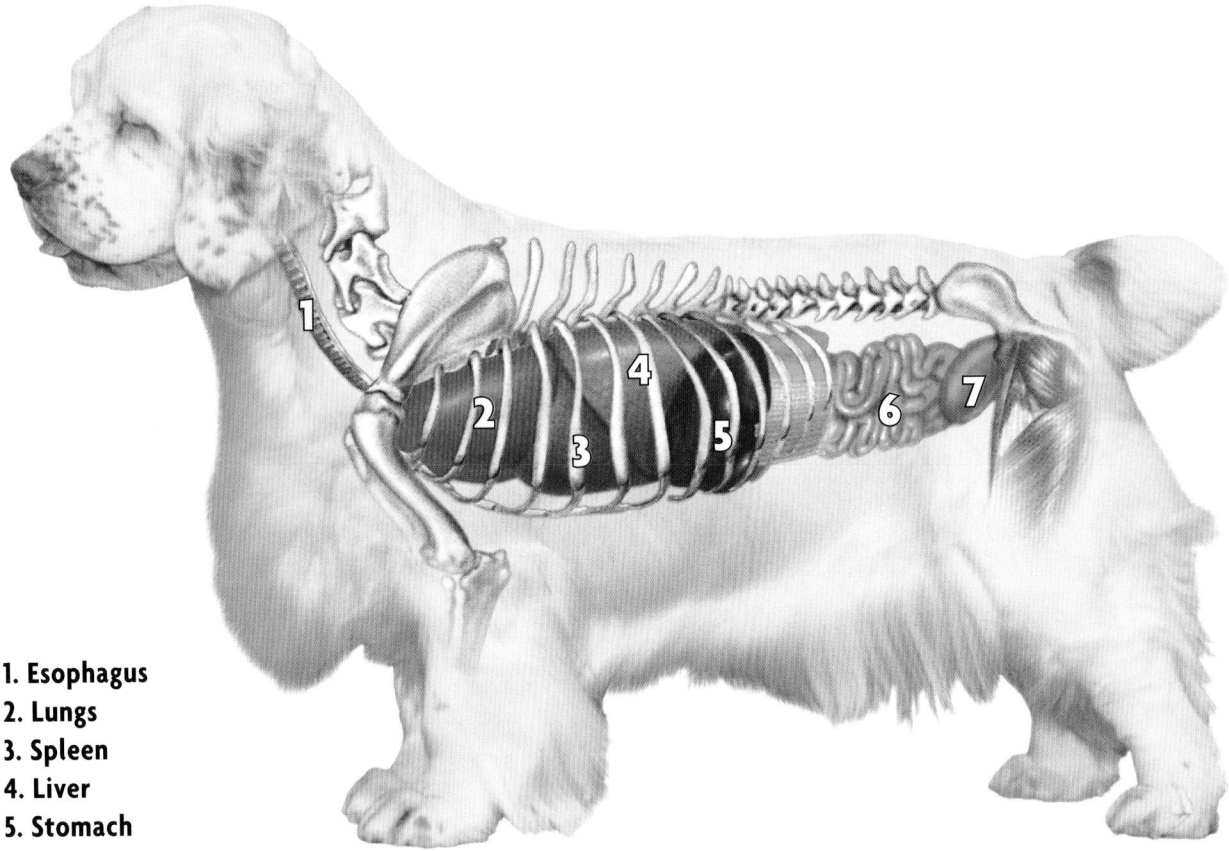

1. Esophagus
2. Lungs
3. Spleen
4. Liver
5. Stomach
6. Intestines
7. Urinary Bladder

available to screen for those problems. Genetic testing offers some important benefits but is available for only a few disorders in a relatively small number of breeds and is not available for some of the most common genetic diseases, such as hip dysplasia, cataracts, epilepsy, cardiomyopathy, etc. This area of research is indeed exciting and increasingly important, and advances will continue to be made each year. In fact, recent research has shown that there is an equivalent dog gene for 75% of known human genes, so research done in either species is likely to benefit the other.

We've also discussed that evaluating the behavioral nature of your Clumber Spaniel and that of his immediate family members is an important part of the selection process that cannot be underestimated or overemphasized. It is sometimes difficult to evaluate temperament in puppies because certain behavioral tendencies, such as some forms of aggression, may not be immediately evident. More dogs are euthanized each year for behavioral reasons than for all medical conditions combined, so it is critical to take temperament issues seriously. Start with a well-balanced, friendly companion and put the time and effort into proper socialization, and you will both be rewarded with a valued relationship for the life of the dog.

Assuming that you have started off with a pup from healthy, sound stock, you then become responsible for helping your veterinarian keep your pet healthy. Some crucial things happen before you even bring your puppy home. Parasite control typically begins at two weeks of age, and vaccinations typically begin at six to eight weeks of age. A pre-pubertal evaluation is typically scheduled for about six months of age. At this time, a dental evaluation is done (since the adult teeth are now in), heartworm prevention is started and neutering or spaying is most commonly done.

It is critical to commence regular dental care at home if you have not already done so. It may not sound very important, but

DENTAL WARNING SIGNS

A veterinary dental exam is necessary if you notice one or any combination of the following in your dog:

- Broken, loose or missing teeth
- Loss of appetite (which could be due to mouth pain or illness caused by infection)
- Gum abnormalities, including redness, swelling and bleeding
- Drooling, with or without blood
- Yellowing of the teeth or gumline, indicating tartar
- Bad breath

Skeletal Structure of the Clumber Spaniel

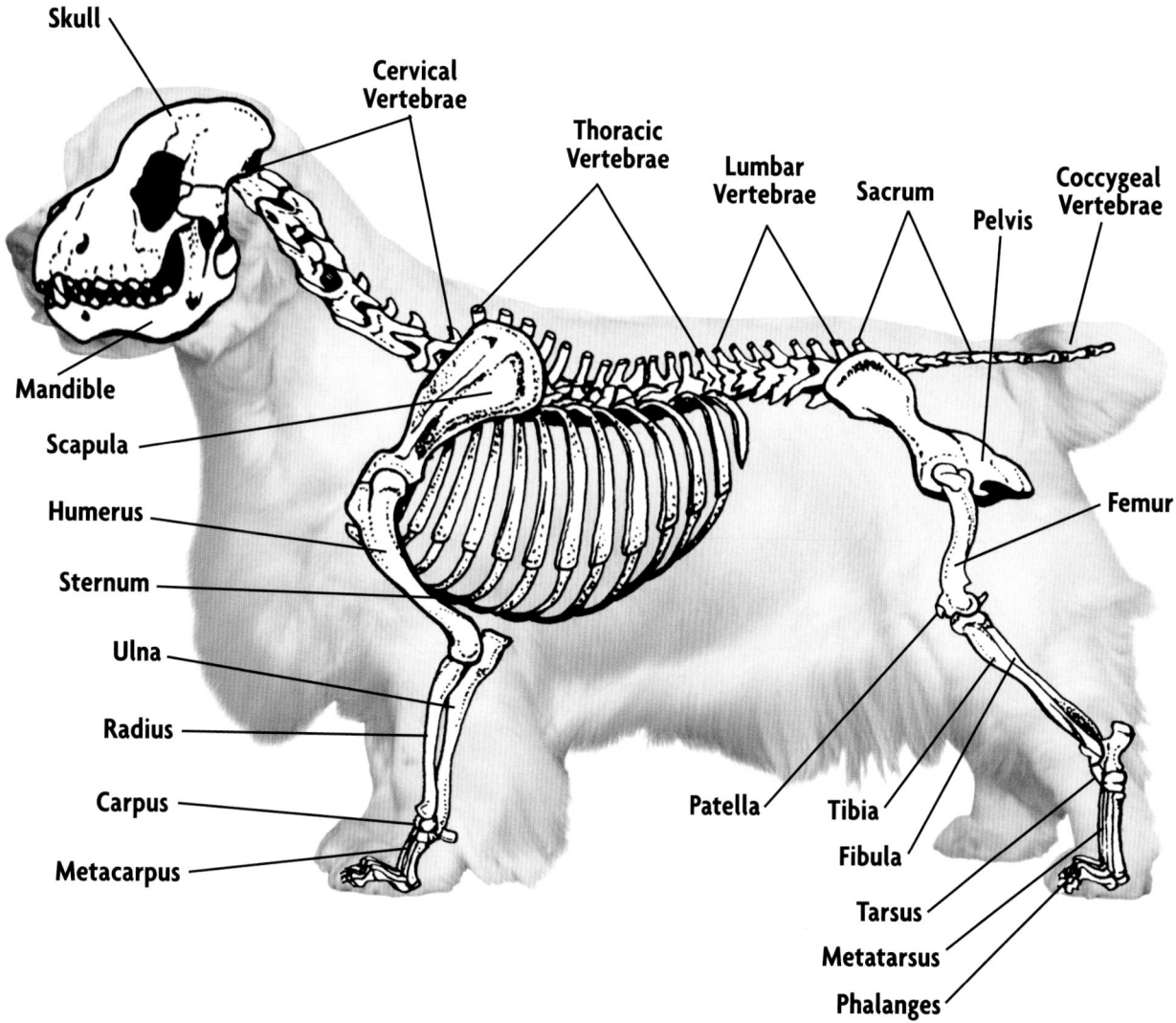

most dogs have active periodontal disease by four years of age if they don't have their teeth cleaned regularly at home, not just at their veterinary exams. Dental exams should be part of every annual physical examination.

Dental problems lead to more than just bad "doggy breath." Gum disease can have very serious medical consequences. If you start brushing your dog's teeth and using antiseptic rinses from a young age, your dog will be accustomed to it and will not resist. The results will be healthy dentition, which your pet will need to enjoy a long, healthy life.

Clumber Spaniels reach adulthood at about two or so years old and true maturity at around age five. Even individual dogs within each breed have different healthcare requirements, so work with your veterinarian to determine what will be needed and what your role should be. This doctor-client relationship is important, because as vaccination guidelines change, there may not be an annual "vaccine visit" scheduled. You must make sure that you see your veterinarian at least annually, even if no vaccines are due, because this is the best opportunity to coordinate healthcare activities and to make sure that no medical issues creep by unaddressed.

When your Clumber Spaniel reaches about three-quarters of his anticipated lifespan, or as deterimined by the vet, he is considered a "senior" and will require some changes to his healthcare routine. In general, if you've been taking great care of your canine companion throughout his formative and adult years, the transition to senior status should be a smooth one. Age is not a disease, and as long as everything is functioning as it should, there is no reason why most of late adulthood should not be rewarding for both you and your pet. This is especially true if you have tended to the details, such as regular veterinary visits, proper dental care, excellent nutrition and management of bone and joint issues.

At this stage in your Clumber Spaniel's life, your veterinarian may want to schedule visits twice yearly, instead of once, to run some laboratory screenings, electrocardiograms and the like, and to change the diet to something more digestible. Catching problems early is the best way to manage them effectively. Treating the early stages of heart disease is so much easier than trying to intervene when there is more significant damage to the heart muscle. Similarly, managing the beginning of kidney problems is fairly routine if there is no significant kidney damage. Other problems, like cognitive dysfunction (similar to senility and Alzheimer's disease), cancer, diabetes and arthritis, are more common in older dogs, but all can be treated to help the dog live as many happy, comfortable years as possible. Just as in people, medical management is more effective (and less expensive) when you catch things early.

SELECTING A VETERINARIAN

There is probably no more important decision that you will make regarding your pet's healthcare than the selection of his doctor. Your pet's veterinarian will be a pediatrician, family-practice physician and gerontologist, depending on the dog's life stage, and will be the individual who makes recommendations regarding issues such as when specialists need to be consulted, when diagnostic testing and/or therapeutic intervention is needed and when you will need to seek outside emergency and critical-care services. Your vet will act as your advocate and liaison throughout these processes.

Everyone has his own idea about what to look for in a vet, an individual who will play a big role in his dog's (and, of course, his own) life for many years to come. For some, it is the compassionate caregiver with whom they hope to develop a professional relationship to span the lives of their dogs and even their future pets. For others, they are seeking a clinician with keen diagnostic and therapeutic insight who can deliver state-of-the-art healthcare. Still others need a veterinary facility that is open evenings and weekends, is in close proximity or provides mobile veterinary services to accommodate their schedules. Your selection of a vet should be based on a combination of things: your trust and confidence in the vet's expertise, knowledge and abilities, as well as his proximity to you. You should be comfortable with the entire staff and with the practice as a whole.

If possible, try to find a vet with Clumber experience. The shape of the Clumber's eyelids is different, with a diamond-shaped lower lid. This sometimes leads to mistaken recommendations for surgical corrections, which may not be needed. Since the Clumber Spaniel is a relatively uncommon breed, vets who are familiar with them are often happy to consult with an owner's vet if the latter is not experienced in the breed.

Just as we have different reasons for selecting our own healthcare professionals (e.g., covered by insurance plan, expert in field, convenient location, etc.), we should not expect that there is a one-size-fits-all recommendation for selecting a veterinarian and veterinary practice. The best advice is to be honest in your assessment of what you expect from a veterinary practice and to conscientiously research the options in your area. You will quickly appreciate that not all veterinary practices are the same, and you will be happiest with one that truly meets your and your Clumber's needs.

There is another point to be considered in the selection of veterinary services. Not that long ago, a single veterinarian would attempt to manage all medical and surgical issues as they arose. That was often problematic, because veterinarians are trained in many species and many diseases, and it was just impossible for general veterinary practitioners to be experts in every species, every breed, every field and every ailment. However, just as in the human healthcare fields, specialization has allowed general practitioners to concentrate on primary healthcare delivery, especially wellness and the prevention of infectious diseases, and to utilize a network of specialists to assist in the management of conditions that require specific expertise and experience. Thus there are now many types of veterinary specialists, including dermatologists, cardiologists, ophthalmologists, surgeons, internists, oncologists, neurologists, behaviorists, criticalists and others to help primary-care veterinarians deal with complicated medical challenges. In most cases, specialists see cases referred by primary-care veterinarians, make diagnoses and set up management plans. From there, the animals' ongoing care is returned to their primary-care veterinarians. This important team approach to your pet's medical-care needs has provided opportunities for advanced care and an unparalleled level of quality to be delivered.

With all of the opportunities for your Clumber Spaniel to receive high-quality veterinary medical care, there is another topic that needs to be addressed at the same time—cost. It's been said that you can have excellent healthcare or inexpensive healthcare, but never both; this is as true in veterinary medicine as it is in human medicine. While veterinary costs are a fraction of what the same services cost in the human healthcare arena, it is still difficult to deal with unanticipated medical costs, especially since they can easily creep into hundreds or even thousands of dollars if specialists or emergency services become involved. However, there are ways of managing these risks. The easiest is to buy pet health insurance and realize that its foremost purpose is not to cover routine healthcare visits but rather to serve as an umbrella for those rainy days when your pet needs medical care

Common Infectious Diseases

Let's discuss some of the diseases that create the need for vaccination in the first place. Following are the major canine infectious diseases and a simple explanation of each.

Rabies: A devastating viral disease that can be fatal in dogs and people. In fact, vaccination of dogs and cats is an important public-health measure to create a resistant animal buffer population to protect people from contracting the disease. Vaccination schedules are determined on a government level and are not optional for pet owners; rabies vaccination is required by law in all 50 states.

Parvovirus: A severe, potentially life-threatening disease that is easily transmitted between dogs. There are four strains of the virus, but it is believed that there is significant "cross-protection" between strains that may be included in individual vaccines.

Distemper: A potentially severe and life-threatening disease with a relatively high risk of exposure, especially in certain regions. In very high-risk distemper environments, young pups may be vaccinated with human measles vaccine, a related virus that offers cross-protection when administered at four to ten weeks of age.

Hepatitis: Caused by canine adenovirus type 1 (CAV-1), but since vaccination with the causative virus has a higher rate of adverse effects, cross-protection is derived from the use of adenovirus type 2 (CAV-2), a cause of respiratory disease and one of the potential causes of canine cough. Vaccination with CAV-2 provides long-term immunity against hepatitis, but relatively less protection against respiratory infection.

Canine cough: Also called tracheobronchitis, actually a fairly complicated result of viral and bacterial offenders; therefore, even with vaccination, protection is incomplete. Wherever dogs congregate, canine cough will likely be spread among them. Intranasal vaccination with *Bordetella* and parainfluenza is the best safeguard, but the duration of immunity does not appear to be very long, typically a year at most. These are non-core vaccines, but vaccination is sometimes mandated by boarding kennels, obedience classes, dog shows and other places where dogs congregate to try to minimize spread of infection.

Leptospirosis: A potentially fatal disease that is more common in some geographic regions. It is capable of being spread to humans. The disease varies with the individual "serovar," or strain, of *Leptospira* involved. Since there does not appear to be much cross-protection between serovars, protection is only as good as the likelihood that the serovar in the vaccine is the same as the one in the pet's local environment. Problems with *Leptospira* vaccines are that protection does not last very long, side effects are not uncommon and a large percentage of dogs (perhaps 30%) may not respond to vaccination.

Borrelia burgdorferi: The cause of Lyme disease, the risk of which varies with the geographic area in which the pet lives and travels. Lyme disease is spread by deer ticks in the eastern US and western black-legged ticks in the western part of the country, and the risk of exposure is high in some regions. Lameness, fever and inappetence are most commonly seen in affected dogs. The extent of protection from the vaccine has not been conclusively demonstrated.

Coronavirus: This disease has a high risk of exposure, especially in areas where dogs congregate, but it typically causes only mild to moderate digestive upset (diarrhea, vomiting, etc.). Vaccines are available, but the duration of protection is believed to be relatively short and the effectiveness of the vaccine in preventing infection is considered low.

There are many other vaccinations available, including those for *Giardia* and canine adenovirus-1. While there may be some specific indications for their use, and local risk factors to be considered, they are not widely recommended for most dogs.

and you don't want to worry about whether or not you can afford that care. There are also third-party medical financial lenders that can be very helpful.

VACCINATIONS AND INFECTIOUS DISEASES

There has never been an easier time to prevent a variety of infectious diseases in your dog, but the advances we've made in veterinary medicine come with a price—choice. Now while it may seem that this choice is a good thing (and it is), it also has never been more difficult for the pet owner (or the vet) to make an informed decision about the best way to protect pets through vaccination.

Years ago, it was just accepted that puppies got a starter series of vaccinations and then annual "boosters" throughout their lives to keep them protected. As more and more vaccines became available, consumers wanted the convenience of having all of that protection in a single injection. The result was "multivalent" vaccines that crammed a lot of protection into a single syringe. The manufacturers' recommendations were to give the vaccines annually, and this was a simple enough protocol to follow. However, as veterinary medicine has become more sophisticated and we have started looking more at healthcare quandaries rather than convenience, it became necessary to reevaluate the situation and deal with some tough questions. It is important to realize that whether or not to use a particular vaccine depends on the risk of contracting the disease against which it protects, the severity of the disease if it is contracted, the duration of immunity provided by the vaccine, the safety of the product and the needs of the individual animal. In a very general sense, rabies, distemper, hepatitis and parvovirus are considered core vaccine needs, while parainfluenza, *Bordetella bronchiseptica*, leptospirosis, coronavirus and borreliosis (Lyme disease) are considered non-core needs and best reserved for animals that demonstrate reasonable risk of contracting the diseases.

NEUTERING/SPAYING

Sterilization procedures (neutering for males/spaying for females) are meant to accomplish several purposes. While the underlying premise is to address the risk of pet overpopulation, there are some medical and behavioral benefits to the surgeries as well. For females, spaying prior to the first estrus (heat cycle) leads to a marked reduction in the risk of mammary cancer and other serious female health problems. There also will be no manifestations of "heat" to

GROWING PAINS

Eosinophilic panosteitis, often known as pano or eopan, is a condition similar to "growing pains." It is frequently seen in adolescent pups between seven and fifteen months of age. It manifests as an intermittent, shifting leg lameness. That is, the dog will be lame on different legs at different times. Diagnosis of this condition by your vet is relatively straightforward, based on physical examination, clinical signs and sometimes x-rays (although typical lesions consistent with this diagnosis often are most noticeable in unaffected legs, making x-ray interpretation a bit more difficult). Although panosteitis can cause puppies to be quite lame, they typically feel fine otherwise, and eating and drinking habits remain normal. Mild pain-killing or anti-inflammatory medicines may bring some comfort, but the true cure for this condition is tincture of time (time itself).

attract male dogs and no bleeding in the house. For males, there is prevention of testicular cancer and a reduction in the risk of prostate problems. In both sexes there may be some limited reduction in aggressive behaviors toward other dogs, and some diminishing of urine marking, roaming and mounting.

While neutering and spaying do indeed prevent animals from contributing to pet overpopulation, even no-cost and low-cost neutering options have not eliminated the problem. Perhaps one of the main reasons for this is that individuals that intentionally breed their dogs and those that allow their animals to run at large are the main causes of unwanted offspring. Also, animals in shelters are often there because they were abandoned or relinquished, not because they came from unplanned matings. Neutering/spaying is important, but it should be considered in the context of the real causes of animals' ending up in shelters and eventually being euthanized.

One of the important considerations regarding neutering is that it is a surgical procedure. This sometimes gets lost in discussions of low-cost procedures and commoditization of the process. In females, spaying is specifically referred to as an ovariohysterectomy. In this procedure, a midline incision is made in the abdomen and the entire uterus and both ovaries are surgically removed. While this is a major invasive surgical procedure, it usually has few complications because it is typically performed on healthy young animals. However, it is major surgery, as any woman who has had a hysterectomy will attest.

In males, neutering has

traditionally referred to castration, which involves the surgical removal of both testicles. While still a significant piece of surgery, there is not the abdominal exposure that is required in the female surgery. In addition, there is now a chemical sterilization option, in which a solution is injected into each testicle, leading to atrophy of the sperm-producing cells. This can typically be done under sedation rather than full anesthesia. This is a relatively new approach, and there are no long-term clinical studies yet available.

Neutering/spaying is typically done around six months of age at most veterinary hospitals, although techniques have been pioneered to perform the procedures in animals as young as eight weeks of age. In general, the surgeries on the very young animals are done for the specific reason of sterilizing them before they go to their new homes. This is done in some shelter hospitals for assurance that the animals will definitely not produce any pups. Otherwise, these organizations need to rely on owners to comply with their wishes to have the animals "altered" at a later date, something that does not always happen.

There are some exciting immunocontraceptive "vaccines" currently under development, and there may be a time when contraception in pets will not require surgical procedures. We anxiously await these developments.

HEALTH ISSUES IN THE BREED

by Roe Froman, DVM

Intervertebral Disc Disease

Long, low and heavy-set, Clumbers are anatomically, if not genetically as well, predisposed to disc disease. In this condition, the cushioning disc between adjacent vertebrae in the spine ruptures or herniates. This puts pressure on the spinal cord, leading to back pain, lameness, reluctance to turn or move the neck and, sometimes, paralysis. Two areas may be affected on Clumbers: the cervical region (neck) or the thoracolumbar area (back). Episodes often manifest as acute onset of pain (reluctance to move, inability to get up, reluctance to turn head or neck, lameness) with periods of remission between flare-ups.

Diagnosis is based upon clinical signs, physical examination, x-rays or myelography (the injection of dye into the spinal canal to identify the exact location of the problem). Treatment is either medical or surgical, depending on location. Cervical discs can respond very well to surgery performed by a practitioner qualified in the procedure. Thoracolumbar disc surgery is most often performed by neurosurgeons. Medical therapy consisting of corticosteroids and

Frolicking about is a most natural behavior for dogs. Sound vertebral health is essential to dogs' being able to act like dogs.

strict crate rest for three weeks is often very helpful.

Immune-Mediated Hemolytic Anemia (IMHA)

IMHA is a very serious, potentially fatal disorder in which the dog's immune system begins attacking its own red blood cells. This can lead to a very sudden anemia. The dog may appear extremely fatigued, unable to rise and not interested in food. The mucous membranes (gums and tissues of the mouth, tissues around the eyes) will be extremely pale and sometimes jaundiced. This is an emergency situation that requires immediate veterinary attention. Aggressive treatment (sometimes necessitating blood transfusions and powerful immunosuppressive drugs) is needed.

Thyroid Disease

Hypothyroidism is not uncommon in Clumber Spaniels. Hypothyroidism is best diagnosed with a complete thyroid panel (*not* just a T4 analysis), including thyroglobulin autoantibody levels. Michigan State University as well as some other veterinary labs can run these complete profiles. Some dogs with elevated autoantibody levels can be treated with low doses of thyroid supplementation, which can help stabilize their bodies' thyroid levels. Clinically hypothyroid dogs are typically overweight, lethargic and heat-seeking, and often have non-itchy hair loss. These signs can be easily corrected with proper supplementation.

Pyruvate Dehydrogenase Deficiency

After an isolated letter to the editor describing four littermates with severe exercise intolerance in a British veterinary journal in the 1970s, this problem has been encountered a few times in various countries in Clumbers. Affected dogs suffer from a genetic deficiency that causes a lack of an enzyme that breaks down waste products produced during muscle activity. This causes a dog to become exhausted very easily, to the point that an affected dog can barely walk around the block. Research is being conducted to completely characterize this problem, to determine the inheritance pattern and to investigate possible therapies. A DNA test is under development for commercial usage at the time of this writing.

FOOD ALLERGIES

Dogs are allergic to many foods that are best-sellers and highly recommended by breeders and veterinarians. Changing the brand of food that you buy may not eliminate the problem if the element to which the dog is allergic is contained in the new brand.

Recognizing a food allergy is difficult. Humans vomit or have rashes when they eat a food to which they are allergic. Dogs neither vomit nor (usually) develop rashes. They react in the same manner as they do to an airborne or flea allergy: they itch, scratch and bite, thus making the diagnosis extremely difficult. While pollen allergies and parasite bites are usually seasonal, food allergies are year-round problems.

It is possible to handle food allergies and food intolerance yourself. This is often accomplished via hypoallergenic diets. It is important for these diets to be nutritionally balanced. They are based on novel carbohydrates and protein sources (ingredients the dog has never eaten before). These may include fish, venison, rabbit, duck and potato. Consult your veterinarian for advice before starting your dog on a new diet. Your vet may also be able to provide you with a completely balanced hypoallergenic diet, whether commercially manufactured or one that requires you to prepare food for the dog. It is also important to avoid incidental protein sources, such as treats or rawhides. Your vet also can advise you about healthy treats that should not cause an allergic reaction.

YOUR DOG NEEDS TO VISIT THE VET IF:

- He has ingested a toxin such as antifreeze or a toxic plant; in these cases, administer first aid and call the vet right away
- His teeth are discolored, loose or missing or he has sores or other signs of infection or abnormality in the mouth
- He has been vomiting, has had diarrhea or has been constipated for over 24 hours; call immediately if you notice blood
- He has refused food for over 24 hours
- His eating habits, water intake or toilet habits have noticeably changed; if you have noticed weight gain or weight loss
- He shows symptoms of bloat, which requires *immediate* attention
- He is salivating excessively
- He has a lump in his throat
- He has a lump or bumps anywhere on the body
- He is very lethargic
- He appears to be in pain or otherwise has trouble chewing or swallowing
- His skin loses elasticity.

Of course, there will be other instances in which a visit to the vet is necessary; these are just some of the signs that could be indicative of serious problems that need to be caught as early as possible.

S. E. M. by Dr. Dennis Kunkel, University of Hawaii

A scanning electron micrograph of a dog flea, *Ctenocephalides canis*, on dog hair.

EXTERNAL PARASITES

Fleas

Fleas have been around for millions of years and, while we have better tools now for controlling them than at any time in the past, there still is little chance that they will end up on an endangered species list. Actually, they are very well adapted to living on our pets, and they continue to adapt as we make advances.

The female flea can consume 15 times her weight in blood during active reproduction and can lay as many as 40 eggs a day. These eggs are very resistant to the effects of insecticides. They hatch into larvae, which then mature and spin cocoons. The immature fleas reside in this pupal stage until the time is right for feeding. This pupal stage is also very resistant to the effects of insecticides, and pupae can last in the environment without feeding for many months. Newly emergent fleas are attracted to animals by the warmth of the animals' bodies, movement and exhaled carbon dioxide. However, when they first emerge from their cocoons, they orient towards light; thus when an animal passes between a flea and the light source, casting a shadow, the flea pounces and starts to feed. If the animal turns out to be a dog or cat, the reproductive cycle continues. If the flea lands on another type of animal, including a person, the flea will bite but will then look for a more appropriate host. An emerging adult flea can survive without feeding for up to 12 months but, once it tastes blood, it can survive off its host for only 3 to 4 days.

It was once thought that fleas spend most of their lives in the environment, but we now know that fleas won't willingly jump off a dog unless leaping to another dog or when physically removed by brushing, bathing or other manipulation. Flea eggs, on the other hand, are shiny and smooth, and they roll off the animal and into the environment. The eggs, larvae and pupae then exist in the environment, but once the adult finds a susceptible animal, it's home sweet home until the flea is forced to seek refuge elsewhere.

Since adult fleas live on the animal and immature forms survive in the environment, a treatment plan must address all stages of the flea life cycle. There are now several safe and effective veterinary spot-on treatments that can be applied on a monthly basis. These include fipronil, imidacloprid, selamectin and permethrin (found in several formulations). Most of these products have significant flea-killing rates within 24 hours. However, none of them will control the immature forms in the environment. To accomplish this, there are a variety of insect growth regulators that can be

FLEA PREVENTION FOR YOUR DOG

- Discuss with your veterinarian the safest product to protect your dog, likely in the form of a monthly tablet or a liquid preparation placed on the back of the dog's neck.
- For dogs suffering from flea-bite dermatitis, a shampoo or topical insecticide treatment is required.
- Your lawn and property should be sprayed with an insecticide designed to kill fleas and ticks that lurk outdoors.
- Using a flea comb, check the dog's coat regularly for any signs of parasites.
- Practice good housekeeping. Vacuum floors, carpets and furniture regularly, especially in the areas that the dog frequents, and wash the dog's bedding weekly.
- Follow up house-cleaning with carpet shampoos and sprays to rid the house of fleas at all stages of development. Insect growth regulators are the safest option.

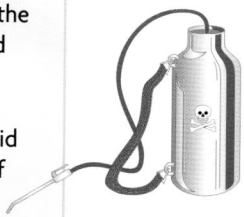

THE FLEA'S LIFE CYCLE

What came first, the flea or the egg? This age-old mystery is more difficult to comprehend than the actual cycle of the flea. Fleas usually live only about four months. A female can lay 2,000 eggs in her lifetime.

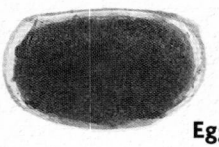

Egg

Photo by Carolina Biological Supply Co.

After ten days of rolling around your carpet or under your furniture, the eggs hatch into larvae, which feed on various and sundry debris. In days or months, depending on the climate, the larvae spin cocoons and develop into the pupal or nymph stage, which quickly develop into fleas.

Larva

Photo by Carolina Biological Supply Co.

Pupa

These immature fleas must locate a host within 10 to 14 days or they will die. Only about 1% of the flea population exist as adult fleas, while the other 99% exist as eggs, larvae or pupae.

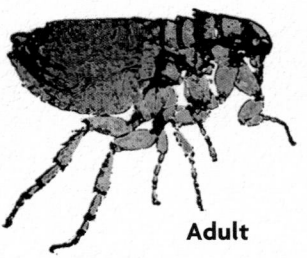

Adult

KILL FLEAS THE NATURAL WAY

If you choose not to go the route of conventional medication, there are some natural ways to ward off fleas:

- Dust your dog with a natural flea powder, composed of such herbal goodies as rosemary, wormwood, pennyroyal, citronella, rue, tobacco powder and eucalyptus.
- Apply diatomaceous earth, the fossilized remains of single-cell algae, to your carpets, furniture and pet's bedding. Even though it's not good for dogs, it's even worse for fleas, which will dry up swiftly and die.
- Brush your dog frequently, give him adequate exercise and let him fast occasionally. All of these activities strengthen the dog's immune system and make him more resistant to disease and parasites.
- Bathe your dog with a capful of pennyroyal or eucalyptus oil.
- Feed a natural diet, free of additives and preservatives. Add a little fresh garlic and brewer's yeast to the dog's morning portion, as these items have flea-repelling properties.

sprayed into the environment (e.g., pyriproxyfen, methoprene, fenoxycarb) as well as insect development inhibitors such as lufenuron that can be administered. These compounds have no effect on adult fleas, but they stop immature forms from developing into adults. In years gone by, we relied heavily on toxic insecticides (such as organophosphates, organochlorines and carbamates) to manage the flea problem, but today's options are not only much safer to use on our pets but also safer for the environment.

Ticks

Ticks are members of the spider class (arachnids) and are blood-sucking parasites capable of transmitting a variety of diseases, including Lyme disease, ehrlichiosis, babesiosis and Rocky Mountain spotted fever. It's easy to see ticks on your own skin, but it is more of a challenge when your furry companion is affected. Whenever you happen to be planning a stroll in a tick-infested area (especially forests, grassy or wooded areas or parks) be prepared to do a thorough inspection of your dog afterward to search for ticks. Ticks can be tricky, so make sure you spend time looking in the ears, between the toes and everywhere else where a tick might hide. Ticks need to be attached for 24–72 hours before they transmit most of the diseases that they carry, so you do have a window of opportunity for some preventive intervention.

A TICKING BOMB

There is nothing good about a tick's harpooning his nose into your dog's skin. Among the diseases caused by ticks are Rocky Mountain spotted fever, canine ehrlichiosis, canine babesiosis, canine hepatozoonosis and Lyme disease. If a dog is allergic to the saliva of a female wood tick, he can develop tick paralysis.

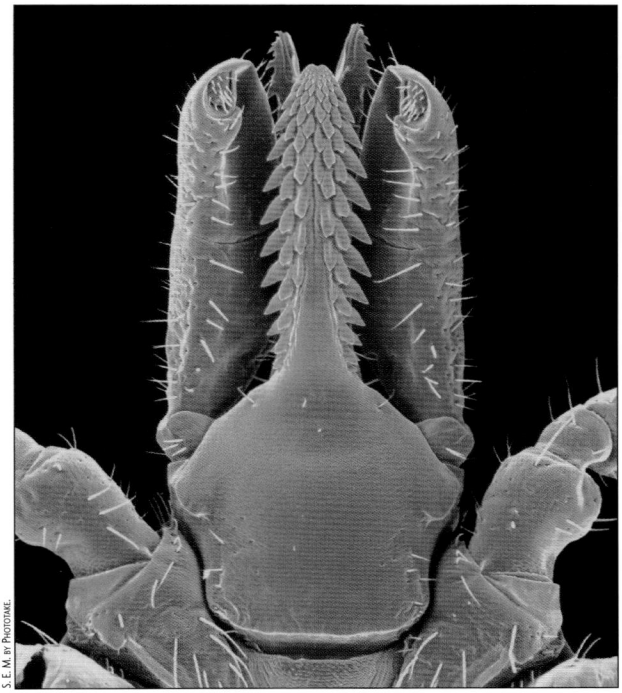

S. E. M. BY PHOTOTAKE.

A scanning electron micrograph of the head of a female deer tick, *Ixodes dammini*, a parasitic tick that carries Lyme disease.

Female ticks live to eat and breed. They can lay between 4,000 and 5,000 eggs and they die soon after. Males, on the other hand, live only to mate with the females and continue the process as long as they are able. Most ticks live on multiple hosts before parasitizing dogs. The immature forms typically reside on grass and shrubs, waiting for susceptible animals to walk by. The larvae and nymph stages typically feed on wildlife.

If only a few ticks are present on a dog, they can be plucked out, but it is important to remove the entire head and mouthparts,

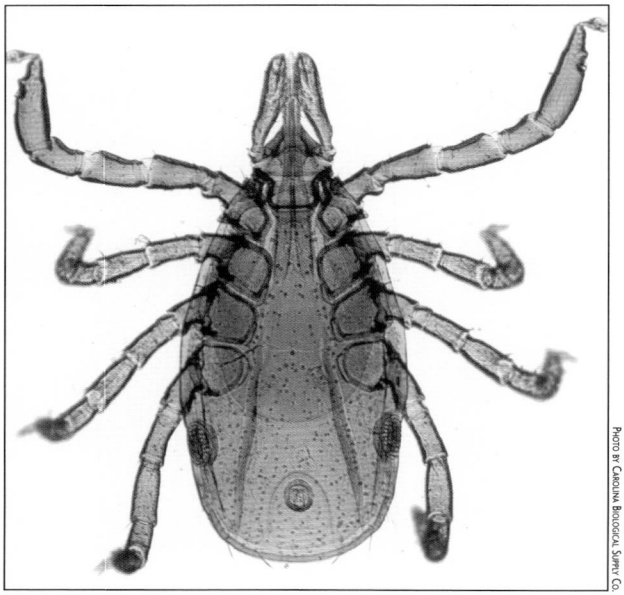

Photo by Carolina Biological Supply Co.

Deer tick, *Ixodes dammini.*

which may be deeply embedded in the skin. This is best accomplished with forceps designed especially for this purpose; fingers can be used but should be protected with rubber gloves, plastic wrap or at least a paper towel. The tick should be grasped as closely as possible to the animal's skin and should be pulled upward with steady, even pressure. Do not squeeze, crush or puncture the body of the tick or you risk exposure to any disease carried by that tick. Once the ticks have been removed, the sites of attachment should be disinfected. Your hands should then be washed with soap and water to further minimize risk of contagion. The tick should be disposed of in a container of alcohol or household bleach.

Some of the newer flea products, specifically those with fipronil, selamectin and permethrin, have effect against some, but not all, species of tick. Flea collars containing appropriate pesticides (e.g., propoxur, chlorfenvinphos) can aid in tick control. In most areas, such collars should be placed on animals in March, at the beginning of the tick season, and changed regularly. Leaving the collar on when the pesticide level is waning invites the development of resistance. Amitraz collars are also good for tick control, and the active ingredient does not interfere with other flea-control products. The ingredient helps prevent the attachment of ticks to the skin and will cause those ticks already on the skin to detach themselves.

TICK CONTROL

Removal of underbrush and leaf litter and the thinning of trees in areas where tick control is desired are recommended. These actions remove the cover and food sources for small animals that serve as hosts for ticks. With continued mowing of grasses in these areas, the probability of ticks' surviving is further reduced. A variety of insecticide ingredients (e.g., resmethrin, carbaryl, permethrin, chlorpyrifos, dioxathion and allethrin) are registered for tick control around the home.

Mites

Mites are tiny arachnid parasites that parasitize the skin of dogs. Skin diseases caused by mites are referred to as "mange," and there are many different forms seen in dogs. These forms are very different from one another, each one warranting an individual description.

Sarcoptic mange, or scabies, is one of the itchiest conditions that affects dogs. The microscopic *Sarcoptes* mites burrow into the superficial layers of the skin and can drive dogs crazy with itchiness. They are also communicable to people, although they can't complete their reproductive cycle on people. In addition to being tiny, the mites also are often difficult to find when trying to make a diagnosis. Skin scrapings from multiple areas are examined microscopically but, even then, sometimes the mites cannot be found.

Fortunately, scabies is relatively easy to treat, and there are a variety of products that will successfully kill the mites. Since the mites can't live in the environment for very long without feeding, a complete cure is usually possible within four to eight weeks.

Cheyletiellosis is caused by a relatively large mite, which sometimes can be seen even without a microscope. Often referred to as "walking dandruff," this also causes itching, but not usually as profound as with scabies.

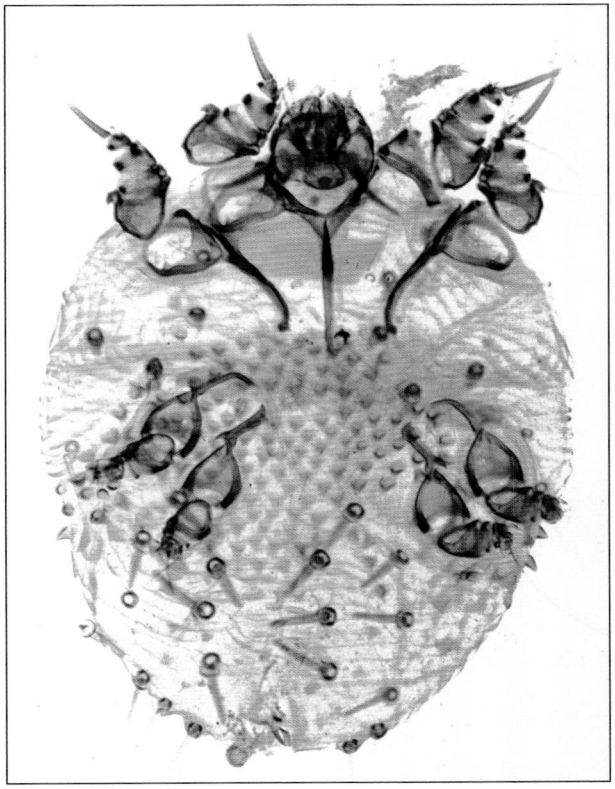

Photo by Phototake.

***Sarcoptes scabiei*, commonly known as the "itch mite."**

While *Cheyletiella* mites can survive somewhat longer in the environment than scabies mites, they too are relatively easy to treat, being responsive to not only the medications used to treat scabies but also often to flea-control products.

Otodectes cynotis is the canine ear mite and is one of the more common causes of mange, especially in young dogs in shelters or pet stores. That's because the mites are typically present in large numbers and are quickly spread to

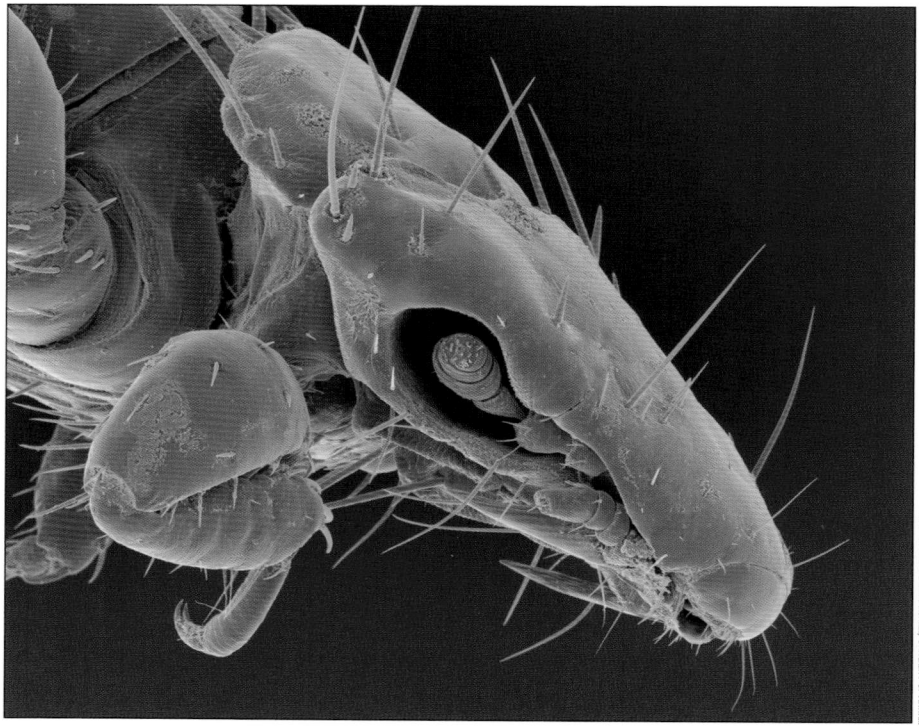

S. E. M. by Dr. Dennis Kunkel, University of Hawaii

Micrograph of a dog louse, *Heterodoxus spiniger*. Female lice attach their eggs to the hairs of the dog. As the eggs hatch, the larval lice bite and feed on the blood. Lice can also feed on dead skin and hair. This feeding activity can cause hair loss and skin problems.

nearby animals. The mites rarely do much harm but can be difficult to eradicate if the treatment regimen is not comprehensive. While many try to treat the condition with ear drops only, this is the most common cause of treatment failure. Ear drops cause the mites to simply move out of the ears and as far away as possible (usually to the base of the tail) until the insecticide levels in the ears drop to an acceptable level—then it's back to business as usual! The successful treatment of ear mites requires treating all animals in the household with a systemic insecticide, such as selamectin, or a combination of miticidal ear drops combined with whole-body flea-control preparations.

Demodicosis, sometimes referred to as red mange, can be one of the most difficult forms of mange to treat. Part of the problem has to do with the fact that the mites live in the hair follicles and they are relatively well shielded from topical and systemic products. The main issue, however, is that demodectic mange typically results only when there is some underlying process interfering with the dog's immune system.

Since *Demodex* mites are

normal residents of the skin of mammals, including humans, there is usually a mite population explosion only when the immune system fails to keep the number of mites in check. In young animals, the immune deficit may be transient or may reflect an actual inherited immune problem. In older animals, demodicosis is usually seen only when there is another disease hampering the immune system, such as diabetes, cancer, thyroid problems or the use of immune-suppressing drugs. Accordingly, treatment involves not only trying to kill the mange mites but also discerning what is interfering with immune function and correcting it if possible.

ILLUSTRATION BY PHOTOTAKE

Illustration of *Demodex folliculoram.*

Chiggers represent several different species of mite that don't parasitize dogs specifically, but do latch on to passersby and can cause irritation. The problem is most prevalent in wooded areas in the late summer and fall. Treatment is not difficult, as the mites do not complete their life cycle on dogs and are susceptible to a variety of miticidal products.

Mosquitoes

Mosquitoes have long been known to transmit a variety of diseases to people, as well as just being biting pests during warm weather. They also pose a real risk to pets. Not only do they carry deadly heartworms but recently there also has been much concern over their involvement with West Nile virus. While we can avoid heartworm with the use of preventive medications, there are no such preventives for West Nile virus. The only method of prevention in endemic areas is active mosquito control. Fortunately, most dogs that have been exposed to the virus only developed flu-like symptoms and, to date, there have not been the large number of reported deaths in canines as seen in some other species.

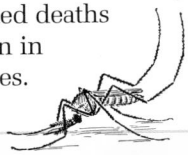

MOSQUITO REPELLENT

Low concentrations of DEET (less than 10%), found in many human mosquito repellents, have been safely used in dogs but, in these concentrations, probably give only about two hours of protection. DEET may be safe in these small concentrations, but since it is not licensed for use on dogs, there is no research proving its safety for dogs. Products containing permethrin give the longest-lasting protection, perhaps two to four weeks. As DEET is not licensed for use on dogs, and both DEET and permethrin can be quite toxic to cats, appropriate care should be exercised. Other products, such as those containing oil of citronella, also have some mosquito-repellent activity, but typically have a relatively short duration of action.

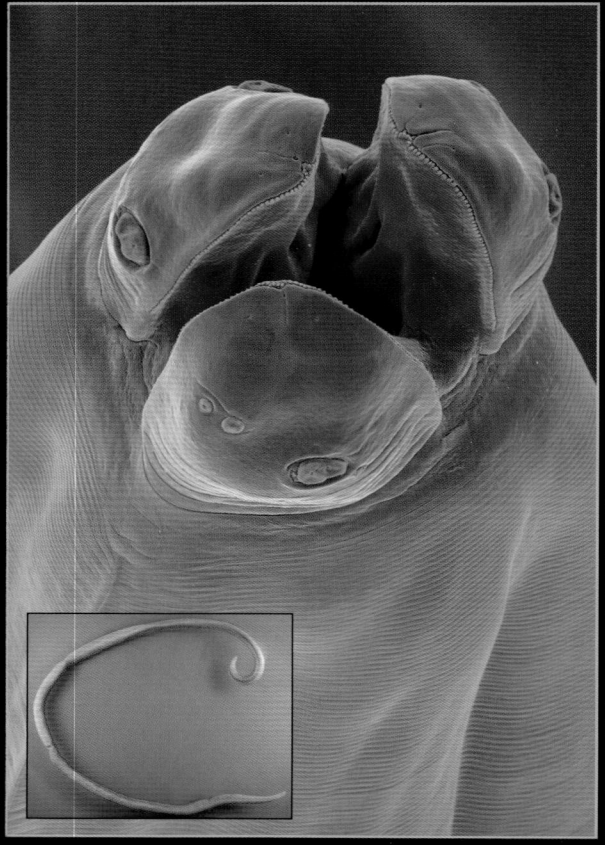

S. E. M. by Dr. Dennis Kinkel, University of Hawaii; Inset by Tam C. Nguyen.

ASCARID DANGERS

The most commonly encountered worms in dogs are roundworms known as ascarids. *Toxascaris leonine* and *Toxocara canis* are the two species that infect dogs. Subsisting in the dog's stomach and intestines, adult roundworms can grow to 7 inches in length and adult females can lay in excess of 200,000 eggs in a single day.

In humans, visceral larval migrans affects people who have ingested eggs of *Toxocara canis*, which frequently contaminates children's sandboxes, beaches and park grounds. The roundworms reside in the human's stomach and intestines, as they would in a dog's, but do not mature. Instead, they find their way to the liver, lungs and skin, or even to the heart or kidneys in severe cases. Deworming puppies is critical in preventing the infection in humans, and young children should never handle nursing pups who have not been dewormed.

The ascarid roundworm *Toxocara canis*, showing the mouth with three lips. INSET: Photomicrograph of the roundworm *Ascaris lumbricoides*.

INTERNAL PARASITES: WORMS

Ascarids

Ascarids are intestinal roundworms that rarely cause severe disease in dogs. Nonetheless, they are of major public health significance because they can be transferred to people. Sadly, it is children who are most commonly affected by the parasite, probably from inadvertently ingesting ascarid-contaminated soil. In fact, many yards and children's sandboxes contain appreciable numbers of ascarid eggs. So, while ascarids don't bite dogs or latch onto their intestines to suck blood, they do cause some nasty medical conditions in children and are best eradicated from our furry friends. Because pups can start passing ascarid eggs by three weeks of age, most internal-parasite-control programs begin at two weeks of age and are repeated every two weeks until pups are eight weeks old. It is

HOOKED ON *ANCYLOSTOMA*

Adult dogs can become infected by the bloodsucking nematodes we commonly call hookworms via ingesting larvae from the ground or via the larvae penetrating the dog's skin. It is not uncommon for infected dogs to show no symptoms of hookworm infestation. Sometimes symptoms occur within ten days of exposure. These symptoms can include bloody diarrhea, anemia, loss of weight and general weakness. Dogs pass the hookworm eggs in their stools, which serves as the vet's method of identifying the infestation. The hookworm larvae can encyst themselves in the dog's tissues and be released when the dog is experiencing stress.

Caused by an *Ancylostoma* species whose common host is the dog, cutaneous larval migrans affects humans, causing itching and lumps and streaks beneath the surface of the skin.

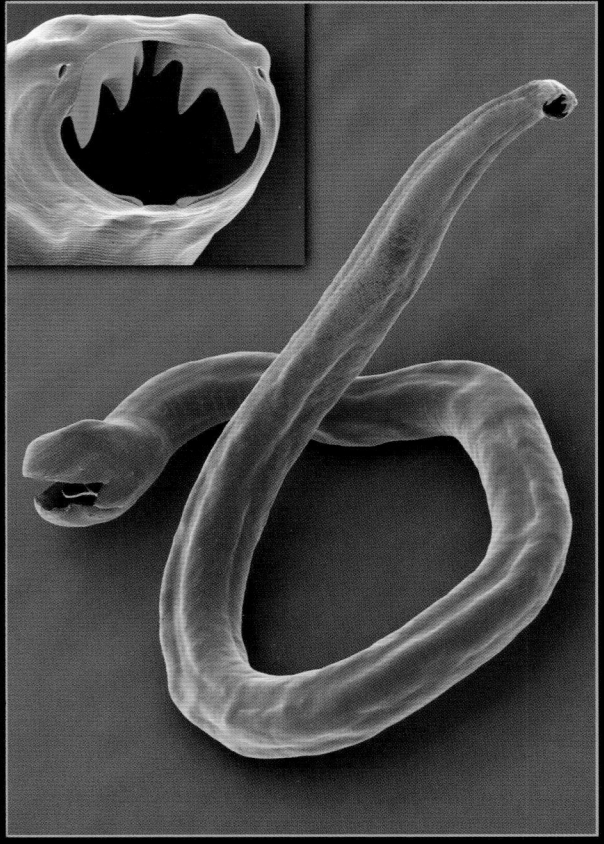

S. E. M. by Dr. Dennis Kunkel, University of Hawaii

The hookworm *Ancylostoma caninum* infests the intestines of dogs. INSET: Note the row of hooks at the posterior end, used to anchor the worm to the intestinal wall.

important to realize that bitches can pass ascarids to their pups even if they test negative prior to whelping. Accordingly, bitches are best treated at the same time as the pups.

Hookworms

Unlike ascarids, hookworms do latch onto a dog's intestinal tract and can cause significant loss of blood and protein. Similar to ascarids, hookworms can be transmitted to humans, where they cause a condition known as cutaneous larval migrans. Dogs can become infected either by consuming the infective larvae or by the larvae's penetrating the skin directly. People most often get infected when they are lying on the ground (such as on a beach) and the larvae penetrate the skin. Yes, the larvae can penetrate through a beach blanket. Hookworms are typically susceptible to the same medications used to treat ascarids.

Whipworms

Whipworms latch onto the lower aspects of the dog's colon and can cause cramping and diarrhea. Eggs do not start to appear in the dog's feces until about three months after the dog was infected. This worm has a peculiar life cycle, which makes it more difficult to control than ascarids or hookworms. The good thing is that whipworms rarely are transferred to people.

Some of the medications used to treat ascarids and hookworms are also effective against whipworms, but, in general, a separate treatment protocol is needed. Since most of the medications are effective against the adults but not the eggs or larvae, treatment is typically repeated in three weeks, and then often in three months as well. Unfortunately, since dogs don't develop resistance to whipworms, it is difficult to prevent them from getting reinfected if they visit soil contaminated with whipworm eggs.

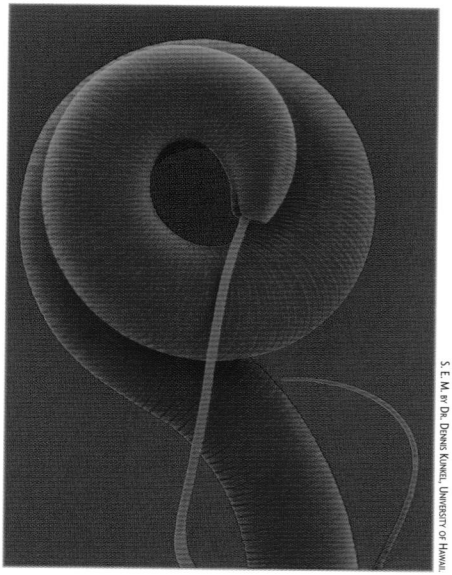

S.E.M. by Dr. Dennis Kunkel, University of Hawaii

Adult whipworm, *Trichuris* sp., an intestinal parasite.

WORM-CONTROL GUIDELINES

- Practice sanitary habits with your dog and home.
- Clean up after your dog and don't let him sniff or eat other dogs' droppings.
- Control insects and fleas in the dog's environment. Fleas, lice, cockroaches, beetles, mice and rats can act as hosts for various worms.
- Prevent dogs from eating uncooked meat, raw poultry and dead animals.
- Keep dogs and children from playing in sand and soil.
- Kennel dogs on cement or gravel; avoid dirt runs.
- Administer heartworm preventives regularly.
- Have your vet examine your dog's stools at your annual visits.
- Select a boarding kennel carefully so as to avoid contamination from other dogs or an unsanitary environment.
- Prevent dogs from roaming. Obey local leash laws.

Tapeworms

There are many different species of tapeworm that affect dogs, but *Dipylidium caninum* is probably the most common and is spread by fleas. Flea larvae feed on organic debris and tapeworm eggs in the environment and, when a dog chews at himself and manages to ingest fleas, he might get a dose of tapeworm at the same time. The tapeworm then develops further in the intestine of the dog.

The tapeworm itself, which is a parasitic flatworm that latches onto the intestinal wall, is composed of numerous segments. When the segments break off into the intestine (as proglottids), they may accumulate around the rectum, like grains of rice. While this tapeworm is disgusting in its behavior, it is not directly communicable to humans (although humans can also get infected by swallowing fleas).

S. E. M. by Dr. Dennis Kunkel, University of Hawaii

A much more dangerous tapeworm is *Echinococcus multilocularis*, which is typically found in foxes, coyotes and wolves. The eggs are passed in the feces and infect rodents, and, when dogs eat the rodents, the dogs can be infected by thousands of adult tapeworms. While the parasites don't cause many problems in dogs, this is considered the most lethal worm infection that people can get. Take appropriate precautions if you live in an area in which these tapeworms are found. Do not use mulch that may contain feces of dogs, cats or wildlife, and discourage your pets from hunting wildlife. Treat these tapeworm infections aggressively in pets, because if humans get infected, approximately half die.

Heartworms

Heartworm disease is caused by the parasite *Dirofilaria immitis* and is seen in dogs around the world. A member of the roundworm group, it is spread between dogs by the bite of an infected mosquito. The mosquito injects infective larvae into the dog's skin with its bite, and these larvae develop under the skin for a period of time before making their way to the heart. There they develop into adults, which grow and create blockages of the heart, lungs and major blood vessels there. They also start producing offspring (microfilariae),

A dog tapeworm proglottid (body segment).

S. E. M. by Dr. Dennis Kunkel, University of Hawaii

The dog tapeworm *Taenia pisiformis*.

A Look at Internal Parasites

Ascarid *Rhabditis*

Photo by Carolina Biological Supply Co.

Hookworm *Ancylostoma caninum*

Photo by Carolina Biological Supply Co.

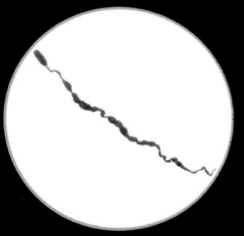

Tapeworm *Dipylidium caninum*

Photo by Tam C. Nguyen.

Heartworm *Dirofilaria immitis*

Photo by Tam C. Nguyen.

and these microfilariae circulate in the bloodstream, waiting to hitch a ride when the next mosquito bites. Once in the mosquito, the microfilariae develop into infective larvae and the entire process is repeated.

When dogs get infected with heartworm, over time they tend to develop symptoms associated with heart disease, such as coughing, exercise intolerance and potentially many other manifestations. Diagnosis is confirmed by either seeing the microfilariae themselves in blood samples or using immunologic tests (antigen testing) to identify the presence of adult heartworms. Since antigen tests measure the presence of adult heartworms and microfilarial tests measure offspring produced by adults, neither are positive until six to seven months after the initial infection. However, the beginning of damage can occur by fifth-stage larvae as early as three months after infection. Thus it is possible for dogs to be harboring problem-causing larvae for up to three months before either type of test would identify an infection.

The good news is that there are great protocols available for preventing heartworm in dogs. Testing is critical in the process, and it is important to understand the benefits as well as the limitations of such testing. All dogs six months of age or older that have not been on continuous heartworm-preventive medication should be

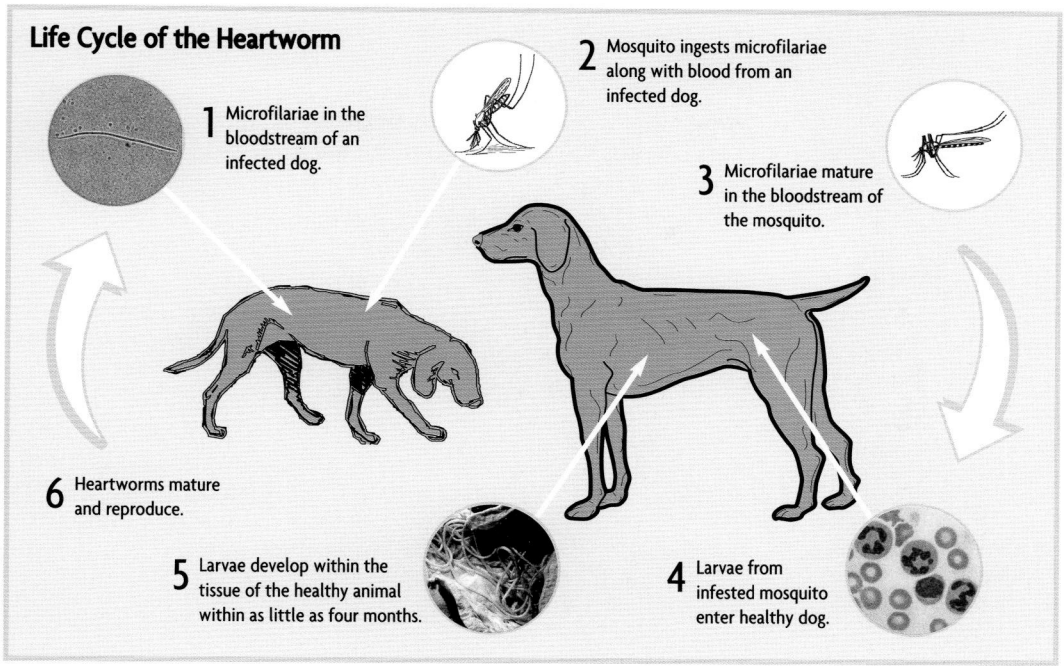

screened with microfilarial or antigen tests. For dogs receiving preventive medication, periodic antigen testing helps assess the effectiveness of the preventives. The American Heartworm Society guidelines suggest that annual retesting may not be necessary when owners have absolutely provided continuous heartworm prevention. Retesting on a two- to three-year interval may be sufficient in these cases. However, your veterinarian will likely have specific guidelines under which heartworm preventives will be prescribed, and many prefer to err on the side of safety and retest annually.

It is indeed fortunate that heartworm is relatively easy to prevent, because treatments can be as life-threatening as the disease itself. Treatment requires a two-step process that kills the adult heartworms first and then the microfilariae. Prevention is obviously preferable; this involves a once-monthly oral or topical treatment. The most common oral preventives include ivermectin (not suitable for some breeds), moxidectin and milbemycin oxime; the once-a-month topical drug selamectin provides heartworm protection in addition to flea, some types of tick and other parasite controls.

THE ABCs OF Emergency Care

Abrasions
Clean wound with running water or 3% hydrogen peroxide. Pat dry with gauze and spray with antibiotic. Do not cover.

Animal Bites
Clean area with soap and saline solution or water. Apply pressure to any bleeding area. Apply antibiotic ointment. Identify animal and contact the vet.

Antifreeze Poisoning
Induce vomiting and take dog to the vet.

Bee Sting
Remove stinger and apply soothing lotion or cold compress; give antihistamine in proper dosage.

Bleeding
Apply pressure directly to wound with gauze or towel for five to ten minutes. If wound does not stop bleeding, wrap wound with gauze and adhesive tape.

Bloat/Gastric Torsion
Immediately take the dog to the vet or emergency clinic; phone from car. No time to waste.

Burns
Chemical: Bathe dog with water and pet shampoo. Rinse in saline solution. Apply antibiotic ointment.

Acid: Rinse with water. Apply one part baking soda, two parts water to affected area.

Alkali: Rinse with water. Apply one part vinegar, four parts water to affected area.

Electrical: Apply antibiotic ointment. Seek veterinary assistance immediately.

Choking
If the dog is on the verge of collapsing, wedge a solid object, such as the handle of a screwdriver, between molars on one side of the mouth to keep mouth open. Pull tongue out. Use long-nosed pliers or fingers to remove foreign object. Do not push the object down the dog's throat. For small or medium dogs, hold dog upside down by hind legs and shake firmly to dislodge foreign object.

Chlorine Ingestion
With clean water, rinse the mouth and eyes. Give the dog water to drink; contact the vet.

Constipation
Feed dog 2 tablespoons bran flakes with each meal. Encourage drinking water. Mix $^{1}/_{4}$-teaspoon mineral oil in dog's food.

Diarrhea
Withhold food for 12 to 24 hours. Feed dog anti-diarrheal with eyedropper. When feeding resumes, feed one part boiled hamburger, one part plain cooked rice, $^{1}/_{4}$- to $^{3}/_{4}$-cup four times daily. Contact vet if persists longer than 24 hours.

Dog Bite
Snip away hair around puncture wound; clean with 3% hydrogen peroxide; apply tincture of iodine. Identify biting dog and contact the vet. If wound appears deep, take the dog to the vet.

Frostbite
Wrap the dog in a heavy blanket. Warm affected area with a warm bath for ten minutes. Red color to skin will return with circulation; if tissues are pale after 20 minutes, contact the vet.

Use a portable, durable container large enough to contain all items.

Heat Stroke
Partially submerge the dog in cold water; if no response within ten minutes, contact the vet.

Hot Spots
Mix 2 packets Domeboro® with 2 cups water. Saturate cloth with mixture and apply to hot spots for 15 to 30 minutes. Apply antibiotic ointment. Repeat every six to eight hours.

Poisonous Plants
Wash affected area with soap and water. Cleanse with alcohol. For foxtail/grass, apply antibiotic ointment. Contact the vet if plant is ingested.

Rat Poison Ingestion
Induce vomiting. Keep dog calm, maintain dog's normal body temperature (use blanket or heating pad). Get to the vet for antidote.

Shock
Keep the dog calm and warm; call for veterinary assistance.

Snake Bite
If possible, bandage the area and apply pressure. If the area is not conducive to bandaging, use ice to control bleeding. Get immediate help from the vet.

Tick Removal
Apply flea and tick spray directly on tick. Wait one minute. Using tweezers or wearing plastic gloves, apply constant pull while grasping tick's body. Apply antibiotic ointment.

Vomiting
Restrict dog's water intake; offer a few ice cubes. Withhold food for next meal. Contact vet if vomiting persists longer than 24 hours.

DOG OWNER'S FIRST-AID KIT

- ❑ Gauze bandages/swabs
- ❑ Adhesive and non-adhesive bandages
- ❑ Antibiotic powder
- ❑ Antiseptic wash
- ❑ Hydrogen peroxide 3%
- ❑ Antibiotic ointment
- ❑ Lubricating jelly
- ❑ Rectal thermometer
- ❑ Nylon muzzle
- ❑ Scissors and forceps
- ❑ Eyedropper
- ❑ Syringe
- ❑ Anti-bacterial/fungal solution
- ❑ Saline solution
- ❑ Antihistamine
- ❑ Cotton balls
- ❑ Nail clippers
- ❑ Screwdriver/pen knife
- ❑ Flashlight
- ❑ Emergency phone numbers

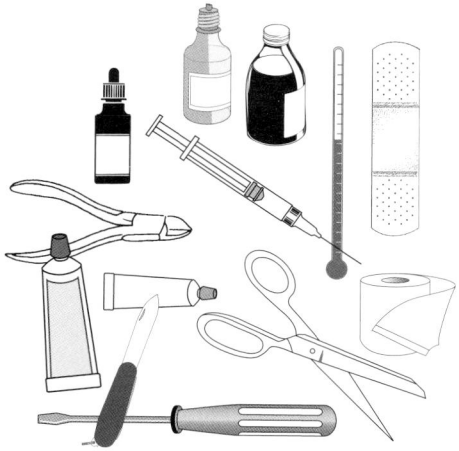

Number-One Killer Disease in Dogs: CANCER

In every age, there is a word associated with a disease or plague that causes humans to shudder. In the 21st century, that word is "cancer." Just as cancer is the leading cause of death in humans, it claims nearly half the lives of dogs that die from a natural disease as well as half the dogs that die over the age of ten years.

Described as a genetic disease, cancer becomes a greater risk as the dog ages. Vets and dog owners have become increasingly aware of the threat of cancer to dogs. Statistics reveal that one dog in every five will develop cancer, the most common of which is skin cancer. Many cancers, including prostate, ovarian and breast cancer, can be avoided by spaying and neutering our dogs by the age of six months.

Early detection of cancer can save or extend a dog's life, so it is absolutely vital for owners to have their dogs examined by a qualified vet or oncologist immediately upon detection of any abnormality. Certain dietary guidelines have also proven to reduce the onset and spread of cancer. Foods based on fish rather than beef, due to the presence of Omega-3 fatty acids, are recommended. Other amino acids such as glutamine have significant benefits for canines, particularly those breeds that show a greater susceptibility to cancer.

Cancer management and treatments promise hope for future generations of canines. Since the disease is genetic, breeders should never breed a dog whose parents, grandparents and any related siblings have developed cancer. It is difficult to know whether to exclude an otherwise healthy dog from a breeding program, as the disease does not manifest itself until the dog's senior years.

RECOGNIZE CANCER WARNING SIGNS

Since early detection can possibly rescue your dog from becoming a cancer statistic, it is essential for owners to recognize the possible signs and seek the assistance of a qualified professional.

- Abnormal bumps or lumps that continue to grow
- Bleeding or discharge from any body cavity
- Persistent stiffness or lameness
- Recurrent sores or sores that do not heal
- Inappetence
- Breathing difficulties
- Weight loss
- Bad breath or odors
- General malaise and fatigue
- Eating and swallowing problems
- Difficulty urinating and defecating

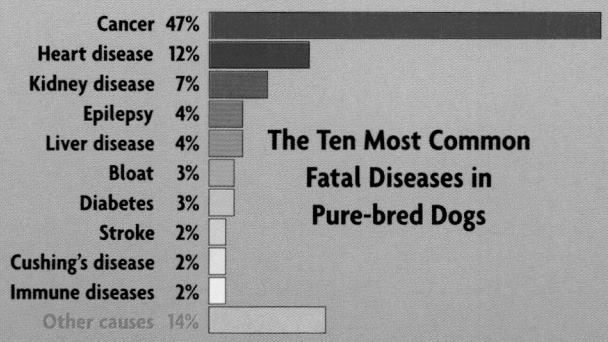

The Ten Most Common Fatal Diseases in Pure-bred Dogs

Canine Cognitive Dysfunction

"Old-Dog" Syndrome

There are many ways for you to evaluate old-dog syndrome. Veterinarians have defined canine cognitive dysfunction as the gradual deterioration of cognitive abilities, indicated by changes in the dog's behavior. When a dog changes his routine response, and maladies have been eliminated as the cause of these behavioral changes, then canine cognitive dysfunction is the usual diagnosis.

More than half the dogs over eight years old suffer from some form of this syndrome. The older the dog, the more chance he has of suffering from it. In humans, doctors often dismiss the canine cognitive dysfunction behavioral changes as part of "winding down."

There are four major signs of canine cognitive dysfunction: frequent potty accidents inside the home, sleeping much more or much less than normal, acting confused and failing to respond to social stimuli.

Symptoms

FREQUENT POTTY ACCIDENTS

- Urinates in the house.
- Defecates in the house.
- Doesn't signal that he wants to go out.

FAILURE TO RESPOND TO SOCIAL STIMULI

- Comes to people less frequently, whether called or not.
- Doesn't tolerate petting for more than a short time.
- Doesn't come to the door when you return home.

CONFUSION

- Goes outside and just stands there.
- Appears confused with a faraway look in his eyes.
- Hides more often.
- Doesn't recognize friends.
- Doesn't come when called.
- Walks around listlessly and without a destination.

SLEEP PATTERNS

- Awakens more slowly.
- Sleeps more than normal during the day.
- Sleeps less during the night.

This is an example of a good eye on a Clumber Spaniel. The eyelids turn neither in nor out; the diamond-shaped lower lid is typical for the breed.

A PET OWNER'S GUIDE TO COMMON OPHTHALMIC DISEASES

by Prof. Dr. Robert L. Peiffer, Jr.

Few would argue that vision is the most important of the cognitive senses, and maintenance of a normal visual system is important for an optimal quality of life. Likewise, pet owners tend to be acutely aware of their pets' eyes and vision, which is important because early detection of ocular disease will optimize therapeutic outcomes. The eye is a sensitive organ with minimal reparative capabilities, and with some diseases, such as glaucoma, uveitis and retinal detachment, early diagnosis and treatment can be critical in terms of whether vision can be preserved.

The causes of ocular disease are quite varied; the nature of dogs makes them susceptible to traumatic conditions, the most common of which include proptosis of the globe, cat scratch injuries and penetrating wounds from foreign objects, including sticks and air-rifle pellets. Infectious diseases caused by bacteria, viruses or fungi may be localized to the eye or part of a systemic infection. Many of the common conditions, including eyelid conformational problems, cataracts, glaucoma and retinal degenerations, have a genetic basis.

Before acquiring your puppy, it is important to ascertain that both parents have been examined and certified as free of eye disease by a veterinary ophthalmologist. Since many of these genetic diseases can be detected early in life, acquire the pup on the condition that he pass a thorough ophthalmic examination by a qualified specialist.

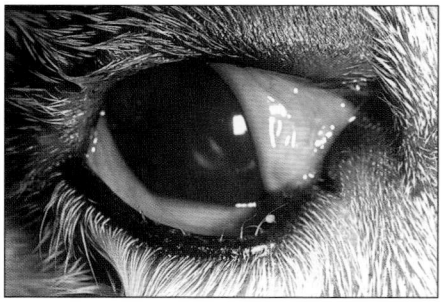

Lower entropion, or rolling in of the eyelid, is causing irritation in the left eye of this young dog. Several extra eyelashes are present on the lower lid, causing a condition known as distichiasis.

Lid Conformational Abnormalities

Rolling in (entropion) or out (ectropion) of the lids tends to be a breed-related problem. Entropion can involve the upper and/or lower lids. Signs usually appear between 3 and 12 months of age. The irritation caused by the eyelid hairs' rubbing

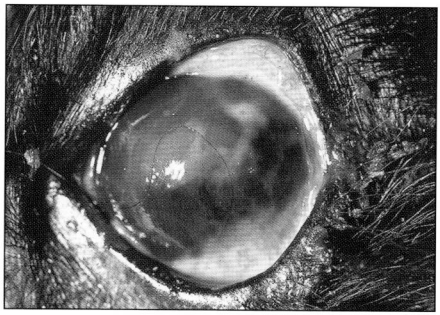

Keratoconjunctivitis sicca, seen here in the right eye of a middle-aged dog, causes a characteristic thick mucous discharge as well as secondary corneal changes.

on the surface of the cornea may result in blinking, tearing and damage to the cornea.

Ectropion is likewise breed-related and is considered "normal" in hounds, for instance; unlike entropion, which results in acute discomfort, ectropion may cause chronic irritation related to exposure and the pooling of secretions. Most of these cases can be managed medically with daily irrigation with sterile saline and topical antibiotics when required.

Eyelash Abnormalities

Dogs normally have lashes only on the upper lids, in contrast to humans. Occasionally, extra eyelashes may be seen emerging at the eyelid margin (distichiasis) or through the inner surface of the eyelid (ectopic cilia).

Conjunctivitis

Inflammation of the conjunctiva, the pink tissue that lines the lids and the anterior portion of the sclera, is generally accompanied by redness, discharge and mild discomfort. The majority of cases are associated with either bacterial infections or dry-eye syndrome. Fortunately, topical medications are generally effective in curing or controlling the problem.

Dry-Eye Syndrome

Dry-eye syndrome (keratoconjunctivitis sicca) is a common cause of external ocular disease. Discharge is typically thick and sticky, and keratitis is a frequent component; any breed can be affected. While some cases can be associated with toxic effects of drugs, including the sulfa antibiotics, the cause in the majority of the cases cannot be determined and is assumed to be immune-mediated.

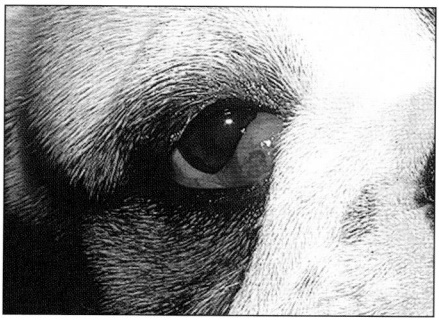

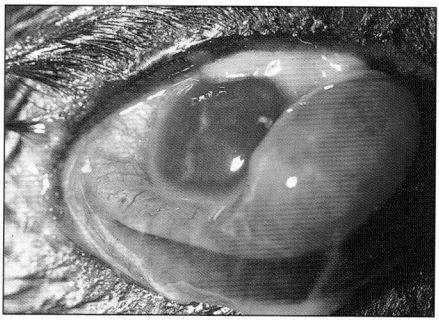

LEFT: Prolapse of the gland of the third eyelid in the right eye of a pup. RIGHT: In this case, in the right eye of a young dog, the prolapsed gland can be seen emerging between the edge of the third eyelid and the corneal surface.

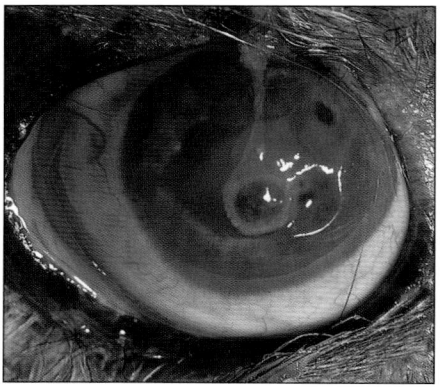

Multiple deep ulcerations affect the cornea of this middle-aged dog.

Prolapse of the Gland of the Third Eyelid

In this condition, commonly referred to as "cherry eye," the gland of the third eyelid, which produces about one-third of the aqueous phase of the tear film and is normally situated within the anterior orbit, prolapses to emerge as a pink fleshy mass protruding over the edge of the third eyelid, between the third eyelid and the cornea. The condition usually develops during the first year of life and, while mild irritation may result, the condition is unsightly as much as anything else.

Corneal Disease

The cornea is the clear front part of the eye that provides the first step in the collection of light on its journey to eventually be focused onto the retina, and most corneal diseases will be manifested by alterations in corneal transparency. The cornea is an exquisitely innervated tissue, and defects in corneal integrity are accompanied by pain, which is demonstrated by squinting.

Corneal ulcers may occur secondarily to trauma or to irritation from entropion or ectopic cilia. In middle-aged or older dogs, epithelial ulcerations may occur spontaneously due to an inherent defect; these are referred to as indolent or Boxer ulcers, in recognition of the breed in which we see the condition most frequently. Infection may occur secondarily. Ulcers can be potentially blinding conditions; severity is dependent upon the size and depth of the ulcer and other complicating features.

Non-ulcerative keratitis tends to have an immune-mediated component and is managed by topical immunosuppressants, usually corticosteroids. Corneal edema can occur in elderly dogs. It is due to a failure of the corneal endothelial "pump."

The cornea responds to chronic irritation by transforming

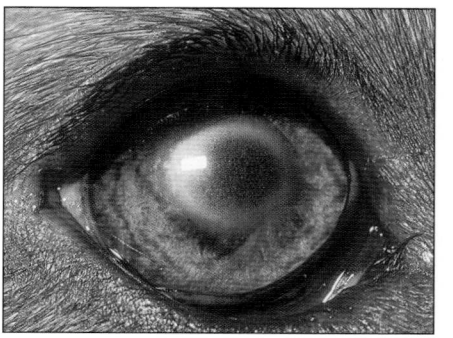

Lipid deposition can occur as a primary inherited dystrophy, or secondarily to hypercholesterolemia (in dogs, frequently associated with hypothyroidism), chronic corneal inflammation or neoplasia. The deposits in this dog assume an oval pattern in the center of the cornea.

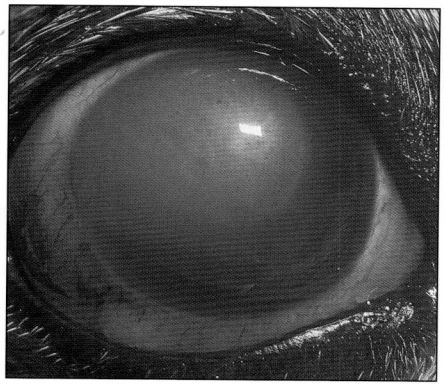

Corneal edema can develop as a slowly progressive process in many breeds as a result of the inability of the corneal endothelial pump to maintain a state of dehydration.

into skin-like tissue that is evident clinically by pigmentation, scarring and vascularization; some cases may respond to tear stimulants, lubricants and topical corticosteroids, while others benefit from surgical narrowing of the eyelid opening in order to enhance corneal protection.

Uveitis

Inflammation of the vascular tissue of the eye—the uvea—is a common and potentially serious disease in dogs. While it may occur secondarily to trauma or other intraocular diseases, such as cataracts, most commonly uveitis is associated with some type of systemic infectious or neoplastic process. Uncontrolled, uveitis can lead to blinding cataracts, glaucoma and/or retinal detachments; aggressive symptomatic therapy with dilating agents (to prevent pupillary adhesions) and anti-inflammatories is critical.

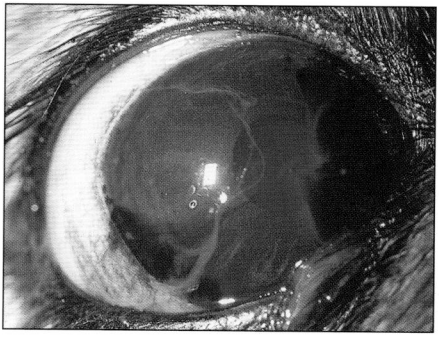

Medial pigmentary keratitis in this dog is associated with irritation from prominent facial folds.

Glaucoma

The eye is essentially a hollow fluid-filled sphere, and the pressure within is maintained by regulation of the rate of fluid production and fluid egress at 10–20 mm of mercury. The retinal cells are extremely sensitive to elevations of intraocular pressure and, unless controlled, permanent blindness can occur within hours to days. In acute glaucoma, the conjunctiva becomes congested, the cornea cloudy, the pupil moderate and fixed; the eye is generally painful and avisual. Increased constant signs of

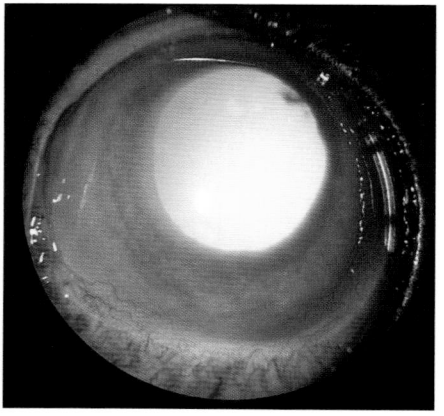

Glaucoma in the dog most commonly occurs as a sudden extreme elevation of intraocular pressure, frequently to three to four times the norm. The eye of this dog demonstrates the common signs of episcleral injection, or redness; mild diffuse corneal cloudiness, due to edema; and a mid-sized fixed pupil.

discomfort will accompany chronic cases.

Management of glaucoma is one of the most challenging situations the veterinary ophthalmologist faces; in spite of intense efforts, many of these cases will result in blindness.

Cataracts and Lens Dislocation

Cataracts are the most common blinding condition in dogs; fortunately, they are readily amenable to surgical intervention, with excellent results in terms of restoration of vision and replacement of the cataractous lens with a synthetic one. Most cataracts in dogs are inherited; less commonly, cataracts can be secondary to trauma or to other ocular diseases, including uveitis, glaucoma, lens luxation and retinal degeneration, or secondary to an underlying systemic metabolic disease, including diabetes and Cushing's disease. Signs include a progressive loss of the bright dark appearance of the pupil, which is replaced by a blue-gray hazy appearance. In this respect, cataracts need to be distinguished from the normal aging process of nuclear sclerosis, which occurs in middle-aged or older animals, and has minimal effect on vision.

Lens dislocation occurs in dogs and frequently leads to secondary glaucoma; early removal of the dislocated lens is generally curative.

Retinal Disease

Retinal degenerations are usually inherited but may be associated

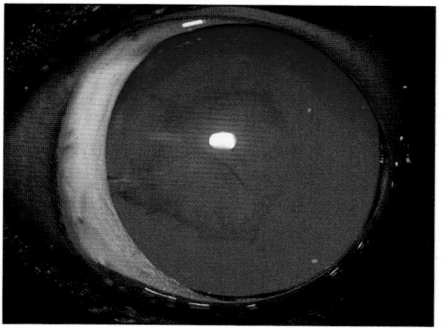

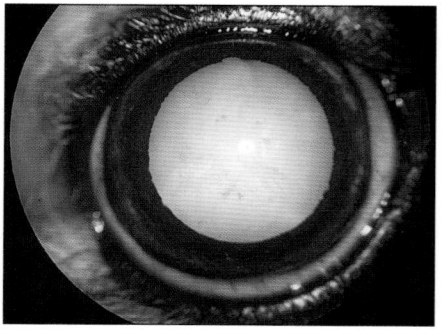

LEFT: The typical posterior subcapsular cataract appears between one and two years of age, but rarely progresses to where the animal has visual problems. RIGHT: Inherited cataracts generally appear between three and six years of age and progress to the stage seen where functional vision is significantly impaired.

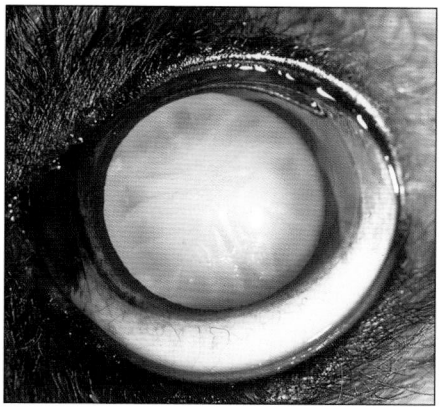

with vitamin E deficiency in dogs. While signs are variable, most frequently one notes a decrease in vision over a period of months, which typically starts out as a night blindness. The cause of a more rapid loss of vision due to retinal degeneration occurs over days to weeks is labeled sudden acquired retinal degeneration or SARD; the outcome, however, is unfortunately usually similar to inherited and nutritional conditions, as the retinal tissues possess minimal regenerative capabilities. Most pets, however, with a bit of extra care and attention, show an amazing ability to adapt to an avisual world and can be maintained as pets with a satisfactory quality of life.

Detachment of the retina—due to accumulation of blood between the retina and the underlying uvea, which is called the choroid—can occur secondarily to retinal tears or holes or tractional forces within the eye, or as a result of uveitis. These types of detachments may be amenable to surgical repair if diagnosed early.

Optic Nerve

Optic neuritis, or inflammation of the nerve that connects the eye with the brain stem, is a relatively uncommon condition that occurs usually with rather sudden loss of vision and widely dilated non-responsive pupils.

Anterior lens luxation can occur as a primary disease in some breeds, or secondarily to trauma. The fibers that hold the lens in place rupture and the lens may migrate through the pupil to be situated in front of the iris. Secondary glaucoma is a frequent and significant complication that can be avoided if the dislocated lens is removed surgically.

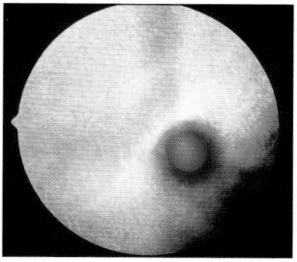

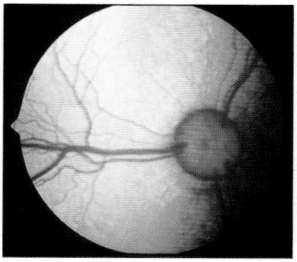

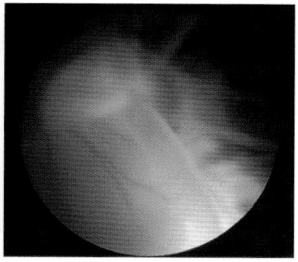

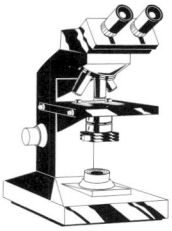

LEFT: The posterior pole of a normal fundus is shown; prominent are the head of the optic nerve and the retinal blood vessels. The retina is transparent, and the prominent green tapetum is seen superiorly.
CENTER: An eye with inherited retinal dysplasia is depicted. The tapetal retina superior to the optic disc is disorganized, with multifocal areas of hyperplasia of the retinal pigment epithelium.
RIGHT: Severe collie eye anomaly and a retinal detachment; this eye unfortunately is blind.

SHOWING YOUR

CLUMBER SPANIEL

Is dog showing in your blood? Are you excited by the idea of gaiting your handsome Clumber Spaniel around the ring to the thunderous applause of an enthusiastic audience? Are you certain that your beloved Clumber Spaniel is flawless? You are not alone! Every loving owner thinks that his dog has no faults, or too few to mention. No matter how many times an owner reads the breed standard, he cannot find any faults in his aristocratic companion dog. If this sounds like you, and if you are considering entering your Clumber Spaniel in a dog show, here are some basic questions to ask yourself:

- Did you purchase a "show-quality" puppy from the breeder?
- Is your puppy at least six months of age?
- Does the puppy exhibit correct show type for his breed?
- Does your puppy have any disqualifying faults?
- Is your Clumber Spaniel registered with the American Kennel Club?
- How much time do you have to devote to training, grooming, conditioning and exhibiting your dog?
- Do you understand the rules and regulations of a dog show?
- Do you have time to learn how to show your dog properly?
- Do you have the financial resources to invest in showing your dog?
- Will you show the dog yourself or hire a professional handler?
- Do you have a vehicle that can

A champion in motion. Handler John Haenszel gaits Ch. Wild Cherry's King of Hearts ("Albert").

It's a family affair: Eileen Heiple with Crystal, Beau and Brit.

Ch. Vishnu Quijote Del Cipres, handled to the Breed win by Douglas Johnson at the 2005 Westminster show.

accommodate your weekend trips to the dog shows?

Success in the show ring requires more than a pretty face, a waggy tail and a pocketful of liver. Even though dog shows can be exciting and enjoyable, the sport of conformation makes great demands on the exhibitors and the dogs. Winning exhibitors live for their dogs, devoting time and money to their dogs' presentation, conditioning and training. Very few novices, even those with good dogs, will find themselves in the winners' circle, though it does happen. Don't be disheartened, though. Every exhibitor began as a novice and worked his way up to the Group ring. It's the "working your way up" part that you must keep in mind.

Assuming that you have purchased a puppy of the correct type and quality for showing, let's begin to examine the world of showing and what's required to get started. The entry fee into a dog show is usually around $25, but there are lots of other hidden costs involved with "finishing" your Clumber Spaniel, that is, making him a champion. Things like equipment, travel, training and conditioning all cost money. A more serious campaign will include fees for a professional handler, boarding, cross-country travel and advertising. Top-winning show dogs can represent a very considerable investment—over $100,000 has been spent in campaigning some dogs. (The investment can be less, of course, for owners who show their own dogs and don't use professional handlers.)

Many owners, on the other hand, enter their "average" Clumber Spaniels in dog shows for the fun and enjoyment of it. Dog showing makes an absorbing hobby, with many rewards for dogs and owners alike. If you're having fun, meeting other people who share your interests and enjoying the overall experience, you likely will catch the "bug." Once the dog-show bug bites, its

FOR MORE INFORMATION...

For reliable up-to-date information about registration, dog shows, parent clubs and other canine competitions for all breeds, contact one of the national registries by mail or via the Internet.

American Kennel Club
5580 Centerview Dr., Raleigh, NC 27606-3390
www.akc.org

Canadian Kennel Club
89 Skyway Ave., Suite 100, Etobicoke,
Ontario M9W 6R4, Canada
www.ckc.ca

The Kennel Club
1-5 Clarges St., Piccadilly,
London W1Y 8AB, UK
www.the-kennel-club.org.uk

Janice Friis showing Ch. Locksley Critter Tintagel ("Picabo") to Best of Winners.

effects can last a lifetime; it's certainly much better than a deer tick! Soon you will be envisioning yourself in the center ring at the Westminster Kennel Club Dog Show in New York City, competing for the prestigious Best in Show cup. This magical dog show is televised annually from Madison Square Garden, and the victorious dog becomes a celebrity overnight. Clumber fanciers were glued to their televisions and ecstatic when Ch. Clussexx Country Sunrise became the first of our breed to win Best in Show at Westminster.

Clumbers in the breed ring, getting stacked and ready to look their best for the judge.

AKC CONFORMATION SHOWING

Getting Started

Visiting a dog show as a spectator is a great place to start. Pick up the judging schedule and show catalog to find out what time your breed is being shown, who is judging the breed and in which ring the classes will be held. To start, Clumber Spaniels compete against other Clumber Spaniels, and the winner is selected as Best of Breed by the judge. This is the procedure for each breed. At a Group show, all of the Best of Breed winners go on to compete for Group One (first place) in their respective groups. For example, all Best of Breed winners in a given group compete against each other; this is done for all seven groups. Finally, all seven Group winners go head to head in the ring for the Best in Show award.

What most spectators don't understand is the basic idea of conformation. A dog show is often referred as a "conformation" show. This means that the judge should decide how each dog stacks up (conforms) to the breed standard for his given breed: how well does this Clumber Spaniel conform to the ideal representative detailed in the standard? Ideally, this is what happens. In reality, however, this ideal often gets slighted as the judge compares Clumber Spaniel #1 to Clumber Spaniel #2. Again, the ideal is that each dog is judged based on his merits in comparison to his breed standard, not in comparison to the other dogs in the ring. It is easier for judges to compare dogs of the same breed to decide which they think is the better specimen; in the Group and Best in Show rings, however, it is very difficult to compare one breed to another, like apples to oranges. Thus the dog's conformation to the breed standard—not to mention advertising dollars and good handling—is essential to success in conformation shows. The dog described in the standard (the standard for each AKC breed is written and approved by the breed's national parent club and then submitted to the AKC for approval) is the perfect dog of that breed, and breeders keep their eye on the standard when they choose which dogs to breed, hoping to get closer and closer to the ideal with each litter.

SHOW POTENTIAL

How possible is it to predict how your ten-week-old puppy will eventually do in the show ring? Most show dogs take a few years to reach their prime, when their bodies are physically mature and their coats are in "full bloom." Experienced breeders, having watched countless pups grow into Best of Breed winners, recognize the glowing attributes that spell "show potential." When selecting a puppy for show, it's best to trust the breeder to recommend which puppy will best suit your aspirations. Some breeders recommend starting with a male puppy, which likely will be more "typey" than his female counterpart.

Another good first step for the novice is to join a dog club. You will be astonished by the many and different kinds of dog clubs in the country, with about 5,000 clubs holding events every year. Most clubs require that prospective new members present two letters of recommendation from existing members. Perhaps you've made some friends visiting a show held by a particular club and you would like to join that club. Dog clubs may specialize in a single breed, or in a specific pursuit, such as obedience, tracking or hunting tests. There are all-breed clubs for all dog enthusiasts; they may sponsor special training days, seminars on topics like grooming or handling or lectures on breeding or canine genetics. There are also clubs that specialize in certain types of dogs, like herding dogs, hunting dogs, companion dogs, etc.

A parent club is the AKC-sanctioned national organization that promotes and safeguards its breed in the country. The Clumber Spaniel Club of America was formed in 1972 and can be contacted on the Internet at www.clumbers.org. The parent club holds an annual national specialty show, usually in a different part of the country each year, where most of the country's top dogs, handlers, exhibitors and breeders gather to compete.

At these specialty shows, only members of a single breed participate. These special events often take place over the course of about a week and include many educational and social events, such as health seminars, extra competitions, breeder forums and parties. Attending a national specialty is the best way to see and appreciate the largest number of examples of a breed, especially in rarer breeds such as the Clumber Spaniel. It is the place to begin to and continue to learn about a breed's history, health and conformation. For novices, attendance at these events can open up a new world of friendship and introduce them to the camaraderie of shared interest in their chosen breed.

MEET THE AKC

The American Kennel Club is the main governing body of the dog sport in the United States. Founded in 1884, the AKC consists of 500 or more independent dog clubs plus 4,500 affiliated clubs, all of which follow the AKC rules and regulations. Additionally, the AKC maintains a registry for pure-bred dogs in the US and works to preserve the integrity of the sport and its continuation in the country. Over 1,000,000 dogs are registered each year, representing about 150 recognized breeds. There are over 15,000 competitive events held annually for which over 2,000,000 dogs enter to participate. Dogs compete to earn over 40 different titles, from Champion to Companion Dog to Master Agility Champion.

How Shows Are Organized

Three kinds of conformation shows are offered by the AKC. There is the all-breed show, in which all AKC-recognized breeds can compete; the specialty show, which is for one breed only and usually sponsored by the breed's parent club and the Group show, for all breeds in one of the AKC's seven groups. The Clumber Spaniel competes in the Sporting Group.

For a dog to become an AKC champion of record, the dog must earn 15 points at shows. The points must be awarded by at least three different judges and must include two "majors" under different judges. A "major" is a three-, four- or five-point win, and the number of points per win is determined by the number of dogs competing in the show on that day. (Dogs that are absent or are excused are not counted.) The number of points that are awarded varies from breed to breed. More dogs are needed to attain a major in more popular breeds, and fewer dogs are needed in less popular breeds. Yearly, the AKC evaluates the number of dogs in competition in each division (there are 14 divisions in all, based on geography) and may or may not change the numbers of dogs required for each number of points. The Clumber Spaniel attracts numerically proportionate representation at all-breed shows.

Only one dog and one bitch of each breed can win points at a given show. There are no "co-ed" classes except for champions of record. Dogs and bitches do not compete against each other until they are champions. Dogs that are not champions (referred to as "class dogs") compete in one of six or seven classes. The class in which a dog is entered depends on age and previous show wins. First there is the Puppy Class (sometimes divided further into classes for 6- to 9-month-olds and 9- to 12-month-olds, and specialty shows sometimes have a 12- to 18-month-old class); next is the Novice Class (for dogs that have no points toward their championships and whose only first-place wins have come in the Puppy Class or the Novice Class, the latter class limited to three first places); then there is the

Each dog's gait is evaluated by the judge. The Clumber should move with effortless drive in the breed's characteristic rolling fashion.

American-bred Class (for dogs bred in the US); the Bred-by-Exhibitor Class (for dogs handled by their breeders or by immediate family members of their breeders) and the Open Class (for any non-champions). Any dog may enter the Open Class, regardless of age or win history, but to be competitive the dog should be older and have ring experience.

The judge at the show begins judging the male dogs in the Puppy Class(es) and proceeds through the other classes. The judge awards first through fourth place in each class. The first-place winners of each class then compete with one another in the Winners Class to determine Winners Dog. The judge then starts over with the bitches,

OPPOSITE PAGE: A first for the Clumber Spaniel in the US: this is Ch. Clussexx Country Sunrise, winning the most prestigious show in the US, the Westminster Kennel Club, in 1996. "Brady" was handled by Jane Alston-Myers, winning under judge D. Roy Holloway.

beginning with the Puppy Class(es) and proceeding up to the Winners Class to award Winners Bitch, just as he did with the dogs. A Reserve Winners Dog and Reserve Winners Bitch are also selected; they could be awarded the points in the case of a disqualification.

The Winners Dog and Winners Bitch are the two that are awarded the points for their breed. They then go on to compete with any champions of record (often called "specials") of their breed that are entered in the show. The champions may be dogs or bitches; in this class, all are shown together. The judge reviews the Winners Dog and Winners Bitch along with all of the champions to select the Best of Breed winner. The Best of Winners is selected between the Winners Dog and Winners Bitch; if one of these two is selected Best of Breed as well, he or she is automatically determined Best of Winners. Lastly, the judge selects Best of Opposite Sex to the Best of Breed winner. The Best of Breed winner then goes on to the Group competition.

At a Group or all-breed show, the Best of Breed winners from each breed are divided into their respective groups to compete against one another for Group One through Group Four. Group One is awarded to the dog that best lives up to the ideal for his breed as described in the standard. A Group judge, therefore, must have a thorough working knowledge of many breed standards. After placements have been made in each group, the seven Group One winners (from the Sporting Group, Toy Group, Hound Group, etc.) compete against each other for the top honor, Best in Show.

There are different ways to find out about dog shows in your area. The American Kennel Club's monthly magazine, the *American Kennel Gazette* is accompanied by the *Events Calendar*; this magazine is available through subscription. You can also look on the AKC's and the Clumber Spaniel Club of America's websites for information and check the event listings in your local newspaper.

Your Clumber Spaniel must be six months of age or older and registered with the AKC in order to be entered in AKC-sanctioned shows in which there are classes for the Clumber Spaniel. Your Clumber Spaniel also must not possess any disqualifying faults and must be sexually intact. The reason for the latter is simple: dog shows are the proving grounds to determine which dogs and bitches are worthy of being bred. If they cannot be bred, that

BEST IN SHOW
THE
WESTMINSTER
KENNEL CLUB

defeats the purpose! On that note, only dogs that have achieved championships, thus proving their excellent quality, should be bred. If you have spayed or neutered your dog, however, there are many AKC events other than conformation, such as obedience trials, agility trials and the Canine Good Citizen® Program, in which you and your Clumber Spaniel can participate.

You're at the Show, Now What? You will fill out an entry form when you register for the show. You must decide and designate on the form in which class you will enter your puppy or adult dog. Remember that some classes are more competitive than others and have limitations based on age and win history. Hopefully you will not be in the first class of the day, so you can take some time watching exactly how the judge is conducting the ring. Notice how the handlers are "stacking" their dogs, meaning setting them up. Does the judge prefer the dogs to be facing one direction or another? Take special note as to how the judge is moving the dogs and how he is instructing the handlers. Is he moving them up and back, once or twice around, in a triangle?

If possible, you will want to get your number beforehand. Your assigned number must be attached as an armband. Do not enter the ring without your number. The ring steward will usually call the exhibits in numerical order. If the exhibits are not called in order, you should strategically place your dog in the line. For instance, if your pup is small for his age, don't stand him next to a large entry; if your dog is reluctant to gait, get at the end of the line-up so that you don't interfere with the other dogs. The judge's first direction, usually, is for all of the handlers to "take the dogs around," which means that everyone gaits his dog around the periphery of the ring.

While you're in the ring, don't let yourself (or your dog) become distracted. Even when you think the judge is not looking at you and your dog, never let your dog stand in an awkward position. The judge could turn to look at you at any time. Concentrate on your dog; he should have your full attention. Stack him in the best way possible. Teach him to free-stand while you hold a treat out for him. Let him understand that he must hold this position for at least a minute before you reward him. Follow the judge's instructions and be aware of what the judge is doing. Don't frustrate the judge by not paying attention to his directions.

When your dog's turn to be judged arrives, keep him steady and calm. The judge will inspect the dog's bite and dentition, overall musculature and structure and, in a male dog, the testicles, which must completely descend into the scrotum. Likewise, the judge will take note of the dog's alertness and temperament. Aggressiveness is a disqualification in most breeds, and so is shyness. A dog must always be approachable by the judge, even if aloofness is one of the breed's characteristics. Once the judge has completed his hands-on inspection, he will instruct you to gait the dog. A dog's gait indicates to the judge that the dog is correctly constructed. Each breed standard describes the ideal correct gait for that breed. After the judge has inspected all of the dogs in the class in this manner, he will ask the entire class to gait together. He will make his final selections after one last look over the class.

Whether you win or lose, the only one disappointed will be you. Never let your dog know that he's not "the winner." Most important is that you reaffirm your dog's love of the game. Reward him for behaving properly and for being the handsome boy or pretty girl that he or she is.

After your first or second experience in the ring, you will know what things you need to work on. Go home, practice and have fun with your Clumber Spaniel. With some time and effort, you and your well-trained show dog will soon be standing in the winners' circle with a blue ribbon!

A win for Ch. Clussexx Billy Goats Gruff at the Roanoke Kennel Club show.

OTHER TYPES OF COMPETITION

In addition to conformation shows, the AKC holds a variety of other competitive events. Obedience trials, agility trials and tracking trials are open to all breeds, while hunting tests, field trials, lure coursing, herding tests and trials, earthdog tests and coonhound events are limited to specific breeds or groups of breeds. Junior Showmanship is offered to aspiring young handlers and their dogs, and the Canine Good Citizen® (CGC) Program is an all-around good-behavior test open to all dogs, pure-bred and mixed. The CGC is a highly recommended program for all dogs, as it encourages the kind of good social behavior that makes dogs more welcome in their neighborhoods and communities. It also underlines the importance of training to allow dogs to fit better into their families and to make the human-canine bond stronger.

Obedience Trials

Mrs. Helen Whitehouse Walker, a Standard Poodle fancier, can be credited with introducing obedience trials to the United States. In the 1930s she designed a series of exercises based on those of the Associated Sheep, Police, Army Dog Society of Great Britain. These exercises were intended to evaluate the working relationship between dog and owner. Since those early days of the sport in the US, obedience trials have grown more and more popular, and now more than 2,000 trials each year attract over 100,000 dogs and their owners. Any dog registered with the AKC, regardless of neutering or other disqualifications that would preclude entry in conformation competition, can participate in obedience trials.

There are three levels of difficulty in obedience competition. The first (and easiest) level is the Novice, in which dogs can earn the Companion Dog (CD) title. The intermediate level is the Open level, in which the Companion Dog Excellent (CDX) title is awarded. The advanced level is the Utility level, in which dogs compete for the Utility Dog (UD) title. Classes at each level are further divided into "A" and "B," with "A" for

CANINE GOOD CITIZEN®

Have you ever considered getting your dog "certified"? The AKC's Canine Good Citizen® Program affords your dog just that opportunity. Your dog shows that he is a well-behaved canine citizen, using the basic training and good manners you have taught him, by taking a series of ten tests that illustrate that he can behave properly at home, in a public place and around other dogs. The tests are administered by participating dog clubs, colleges, 4-H clubs, Scouts and other community groups and are open to all pure-bred and mixed-breed dogs. Upon passing the ten tests, the suffix CGC is then applied to your dog's name.

The ten tests are: 1. Accepting a friendly stranger; 2. Sitting politely for petting; 3. Appearance and grooming; 4. Walking on a lead; 5. Walking through a group of people; 6. Sit, down and stay on command; 7. Coming when called; 8. Meeting another dog; 9. Calm reaction to distractions; 10. Separation from owner.

This marvelously trained Clumber Spaniel is clearing the bar jump at an obedience trial.

beginners and "B" for those with more experience. In order to win a title at a given level, a dog must earn three "legs." A "leg" is accomplished when a dog scores 170 or higher (200 is a perfect score). The scoring system gets a little trickier when you understand that a dog must score more than 50% of the points available for each exercise in order to actually earn the points. Available points for each exercise range between 20 and 40.

A dog must complete different exercises at each level of obedience. The Novice exercises are the easiest, with the Open and finally the Utility levels progressing in difficulty. Examples of Novice exercises are on- and off-lead heeling, a figure-8 pattern, performing a recall (or come), long sit and long down and standing for examination. In the Open level, the Novice-level exercises are required again, but this time without a leash and for longer durations. In addition, the dog must clear a broad jump, retrieve over a jump and drop on recall. In the Utility level, the exercises are quite difficult, including executing basic commands based on hand signals, following a complex heeling pattern, locating articles based on scent discrimination and completing jumps at the handler's direction.

To compete in obedience trials, the Clumber Spaniel must be able to follow the handler's commands without fail. Note how attentive this Clumber is to his master's next move.

Once he's earned the UD title, a dog can go on to win the prestigious title of Utility Dog Excellent (UDX) by winning "legs" in ten shows. Additionally, Utility Dogs who win "legs" in Open B and Utility B earn points toward the lofty title of Obedience Trial Champion (OTCh.). Established in 1977 by the AKC, this title requires a dog to earn 100 points as well as three first places in a combination of Open B and Utility B classes under three different judges. The "brass ring" of obedience competition is the AKC's National Obedience Invitational. This is an exclusive competition for only the cream of the obedience crop. In order to qualify for the invitational, a dog must be ranked in either the top 25 all-breeds in obedience or in the top three for his breed in obedience. The title at stake here is that of National Obedience Champion (NOC).

Agility Trials

Agility trials became sanctioned by the AKC in August 1994, when the first licensed agility trials were held. Since that time, agility certainly has grown in popularity by leaps and bounds, literally! The AKC allows all registered breeds (including Miscellaneous Class breeds) to participate, providing the dog is 12 months of age or older. Agility is designed so that the handler demonstrates how well the dog can work at his side. The handler directs his dog through, over, under and around an obstacle course that includes jumps, tires, the dog walk, weave poles, pipe tunnels, collapsed tunnels and more. While working his way through the course, the dog must keep one eye and ear on the handler and the rest of his body on the course. The handler runs along with the dog, giving verbal and hand signals to guide the dog through the course.

The first organization to promote agility trials in the US was the United States Dog Agility Association, Inc.

(USDAA). Established in 1986, the USDAA sparked the formation of many member clubs around the country. To participate in USDAA trials, dogs must be at least 18 months of age.

The USDAA and AKC both offer titles to winning dogs, although the exercises and requirements of the two organizations differ. Agility Dog (AD), Advanced Agility Dog (AAD) and Master Agility Dog (MAD) are the titles offered by the USDAA, while the AKC offers Novice Agility (NA), Open Agility (OA), Agility Excellent (AX) and Master Agility Excellent (MX). Beyond these four AKC titles, dogs can win additional titles in "jumper" classes: Jumper with Weave Novice (NAJ), Open (OAJ) and Excellent (MXJ). The ultimate title in AKC agility is MACH, Master Agility Champion. Dogs can continue to add number designations to the MACH title, indicating how many times the dog has met the title's requirements (MACH1, MACH2 and so on).

Agility trials are a great way to keep your dog active, and they will keep you running, too! You should join a local agility club to learn more about the sport. These clubs offer sessions in which you can introduce your dog to the various obstacles as well as training classes to prepare him for competition. In no time, your dog will be climbing A-frames, crossing the dog walk and flying over hurdles, all with you

Across the dog walk...

On the way down...

And off and running, on to conquer the next obstacle!

Here's Am./Can. Ch. Critter's Hungry Heart TD, CD, JH, CGC, showing off his remarkable nose. Clumbers make fine tracking dogs and prove to be consistent, persistent performers.

right beside him. Your heart will leap every time your dog jumps through the hoop—and you'll be having just as much (if not more) fun!

Tracking

Tracking tests are exciting ways to test your Clumber Spaniel's instinctive scenting ability on a competitive level. All dogs have a nose, and all breeds are welcome in tracking tests. Clumbers enjoy working for tracking titles and are quite good at it. The first AKC-licensed tracking test took place in 1937 as part of the Utility level at an obedience trial, and thus competitive tracking was officially begun. The first title, Tracking Dog (TD), was offered in 1947, ten years after the first official tracking test. It was not until 1980 that the AKC added the title Tracking Dog Excellent (TDX), which was followed by the title Variable Surface Tracking (VST) in 1995. Champion Tracker (CT) is awarded to a dog who has earned all three of those titles.

Am./Can. Ch. Raycroft Springsteen TD is a handsome and accomplished Clumber from the Great Lakes region of the country. The suffix TD is an American Kennel Club title for Tracking Dog.

The TD level is the first and most basic level in tracking, progressing in difficulty to the TDX and then the VST. A dog must follow a track laid by a human 30 to 120 minutes prior in order to earn the TD title. The track is about 500 yards long and contains up to 5 directional changes. At the next level, the TDX, the dog must follow a 3- to 5-hour-old track over a course that is up to 1,000 yards long and has up to 7 directional changes. In the most difficult level, the VST, the track is up to 5 hours old and located in an urban setting.

Hunting Tests

Hunting tests are not competitive like field trials, and participating dogs are judged against a standard, as in a conformation show. Clumber Spaniels are eligible to participate in hunting tests, and they particularly enjoy the work that they were bred to do. At this time there are 48 Clumber Spaniels who have earned hunting titles. The first hunting tests were devised by the North American Hunting Retriever Association (NAHRA) as an alternative to field trials for retriever owners to appreciate their dogs' natural innate ability in the field without the expense and pressure of a formal field trial. The intent of hunting tests is the same as that of field trials: to test the dog's ability in a simulated hunting scenario.

The AKC instituted its hunting tests in June 1985; since then, their popularity has grown tremendously. The AKC offers three titles at hunting tests, Junior Hunter (JH), Senior Hunter (SH) and Master Hunter (MH). Each title requires that the dog earn qualifying "legs" at the tests: the JH requiring four; the SH, five; and the MH, six.

Bob Wickwire and Maddie relax and get cleaned up after a day on the hunt.

Am./Can. Ch. Flyaway Corey's John Glenn CGC, WDX, MH, known as "Herschel," is an active hunter with his owner and in competition. Just a week after winning a gundog specialty, he poses with the fruits of his day's labor in the field.

INDEX

*Page numbers in **boldface** indicate illustrations.*

Acetaminophen 59
Activities 16, 26, 99
Activity level 20, 66
Adenovirus 108
Adult dog
—adoption 34, 78
—feeding 63
—health 105
—training 77-79
Aggression 56, 79, 95, 110
Agility 16, 26, 99, 148, 150, 153
Aging 105
Albert **138**
Albert, Prince 11
All-breed show 146
Allergy to food 113
Alpha role 77, 87
Alpine Spaniels 11
Alston-Myers, Jane 14
American Heartworm Society 127
American Kennel Club 14, 15, 139, 140, 142-155
—breed standard 29
—conformation showing 142-150
—other competitive events 148, 150-155
—recognition of breed 11
American Kennel Gazette 146
Amity **21**
Anal glands 74
Ancylostoma caninum **123**, **126**
Andronicus kennel 12
Andronicus Winchester 12
Anemia 112
Annual vet exams 105
Antifreeze 52
Appetite loss 103
Ascarid **122**, 123
Ascaris lumbricoides **122**
Attention 88, 89, 95
Back problems 27, 111
Barber, C. Burton 9
Basset Hound 9
Barking 22
Bathing 68, 70
Beau **80**, **85**, **139**
Bedding 45, 54, 84
Best of Breed 146
Best of Opposite Sex 146
Best of Winners 146
Best in Show 146
Binks, Reuben Ward 12
Bite 39
Blenheim Spaniel 10
BlueMoon 16
Body language 79, 85, 91
Bones 46, 65
Bordetella 108, 109
Borrelia burgdorferi 108
Borreliosis 109
Bowls 43
Brady 14, 15, **16**, 141, **147**
Breakaway 15
Breed clubs 13, 15, 16, 29, 34, 35, 143
Breeder 34-41, 101, 143
Brit **85**, **139**
Brushing 68
Brutus **21**
Cameo 15
Canada 11, 140
Cancer 109, 110, 130
Canine cough 108
Canine development schedule 82
Canine Good Citizen® 148, 150
Car travel 53, 76, 95
Carnforth kennels 12
Cataracts **136**
Cavalier King Charles Spaniel 10
Champion 144
Cherry eye **133**, 134
Chew toys 46-48, 51, 59, 84
Chewing 45, 46, 51, 58, 95
Cheyletiella mite **119**
Chiggers 121
Children 20-21, 27, 53, 55, 59, 79, 95
Class dogs 145
Classes at shows 145
Cleo **21**
Clumber Park 8
Clumber roll 25
Clumber Spaniel Club of America 13, 15, 16, 29, 34, 35, 143
Clumber Spaniel Fanciers of Michigan 13
Clussexx Billy Goats Gruff 15, **149**
Clussexx Country Sunrise 14, 15, **16**, 141, **147**
Clussexx kennels 15
Clussexx Marry Me Bill 15
Clussexx Overdue Bill 15
Coat 23
Cognitive dysfunction 105, 131
Collar 48-50, 75, 88, 95
Collie eye 137
Come 94
Commands 58, 81, 90-97
Commitment of ownership 25-26, 28, 33, 40-42
Companionway 15
Competitive events 16, 26, 148, 150
Conformation showing 142-150
—awards 142, 146
—classes 145
—ring procedure 149
Conjunctivitis 133
Consistency 56, 58, 90, 92
Core vaccines 109
Corneal disease **134-135**
Coronavirus 108, 109
Correction 88
Crate 44-45, 53-54, 60, 83
—pads 45
—training 44, 80-87
Critter 15
Critter's Hungry Heart **154**
Critter's Leap of Faith **41**
Crufts Dog Show 15
Crying 54, 60, 84
Crystal **85**, **139**
Ctenocephalides canis **114**
Cypress Woods Certified Copy **31**
Cypress Woods kennel 14-15
Dangers in the home 50-52, 59, 81
DEET 121
Deke **21**
Demodex mite **121**
Demodicosis 120-121
Dental health 73, 103, 105
Diet 61-65
Dipylidium caninum 124, **126**
Dirofilaria immitis 125, **126**, **127**
Discipline 57, 87
Distemper 108-109
Distichiasis **132**, 133
Docking tails 25
Dogfight 95
Dominance 90, 97
Down 85, 91
Down/stay 93
Drumhill 15
Dry eye 27, **133**
Du Pont, Mr. and Mrs. S. Hallock 11
Ear
—cleaning 71
—mite infestation 72, 119-120
Earthdog tests 150
Echinococcus multilocularis 125
Ectopic cilia 133
Ectropion 132
Eggs 65
Emergency care 128-129
Emma **21**
England 8-10, 11
Entropion **132**
Eosinophilic panosteitis 110
Estrus 109
Europe 8
Events Calendar 146
Excessive thirst 66
Exercise 21, 66
—pen 81
Expression 23
External parasites 114-121
Eyelash abnormalities 133
Eyelid abnormalities 134
Eyes
—care of 73
—diseases of 27, 132-137
Family dog 20, 25-26
Family meeting the puppy 53
Farrow, James 10
Fear 56
—period 55
Feeding 61-65
Fenced yard 26, 33, 51, 95
First aid 128-129
First night in new home 54
Fleas **114**, 115, **116**
Flushing 9, 22
Flyaway Corey's John Glenn **21**, **155**
Food 61-65, 83, 113
—allergy 113
—bowls 43
—intolerance 113
—loss of interest in 103
—raw 65
—rewards 77, 87, 97, 99
—toxic to dogs 64, 65
France 8, 9
Freeman, Dr. Bryant 13
French Revolution 9-10
Gait 25, 149
Genetic
—problems 27
—testing 101, 103
Giardia 108
Gies, Eunice and Milton 12
Glaucoma 135, **136**
Grooming 68-74
Group competition 142-143, 146
Gum disease 105
Handler 139
Haverick, Jeane 15
Health 52
—adult dog 105
—considerations 27
—insurance for pets 107
—journal 52
—puppy 35, 103
—senior dog 105
Heart disease 105
Heartworm 103, 125, **126**, **127**
Heat cycle 109
Heel 95-97
Height 25
Hepatitis 108, 109
Hereditary problems 27, 111
Herschel **21**, **155**
Heterodoxus spiniger **120**
Hip dysplasia 27
Hookworm **123**, **126**
Homemade toys 48
House-training 44, 80-87
Hunting 16, 19, 22
—early packs 9, 11-12
—events 99, 150, 155
—Retriever Club 155
Hypothyroidism 27, 112
Identification 74-76
Immune-mediated hemolytic anemia 27, 112
Infectious diseases 108, 109
Insurance 107

Internal parasites 122-127
Intervertebral disc disease 27, 111
Ironside, Bill 15
Ixodes dammini **117-118**
Jetset's Deke Slayton **8, 14**
Johnson, Douglas A. 15
Judges 144, 146, 149
Jumping up 18, 85
Junior **25**
Junior Showmanship 150
Kennel Club, The 140
Keratoconjunctivitis sicca 27, **133**
Kidney problems 105
Klondike **85**
Lameness 110
Lapis **12**
Leash 50, 84, 88, 97
Leave it 95
Length of body 25
Lens problems 136, **137**
Leptospirosis 108, 109
Lid conformational abnormalities 132
Lifespan 27, 33, 105
Lipid deposition **134**
Liver 65
Locksley Critter Tintagel **141**
Lollypop **21**
Lost dog 75
Lothian 16
Louse **120**
Loyalty 25
Lure coursing 150
Lyme disease 108, 109
Maddie **21**, **155**
Majors 144
Maturity 65, 105
Meat 65
Medial pigmentary keratitis 135
Michigan State University 112
Microchip 75
Milk 65
Mites **119**, 120, **121**
Mosquitoes 121, 125, 127
Mounting 110
Nail clipping 70
National Obedience Champion 152
National specialty 14, 15, 143-144
Navarre 11
Neck problems 27
Neutering 103, 109-111, 148
New Keeper, The 9
Newcastle, Duke of 8-9
Nexus 15
Nipping 58
Noailles, Duc de 9
Non-core vaccines 109
North American Hunting Retriever Association 155
Oakerland Repeater **11**
Obedience 16, 21, 26, 92
—classes 97-98
—trials 99, 148, 150
Off 85
Okay 92, 97
Old-dog syndrome 105, 131
Optic neuritis 137
Origin of breed
—English theories 9-10
—French theory 9
—Spanish theory 11
Other dogs 110
Other pets 79
Otodectes cynotis 129
Outdoor safety 26, 33, 50-52, 95
Ovariohysterectomy 110
Ownership 25-26, 28, 33, 40-42
Pachon 11
Pack animals 56, 77, 87
Panosteitis 110
Paper-training 80, 85
Parainfluenza 108-109
Parasite
—control 103
—external 114-121
—internal 122-127
Parent club 13, 15, 16, 29, 34, 35, 143
Parvovirus 108-109
Patience 78
Pedigree 39, 42
Performance events 16, 26, 150-155
Personality 17-23
Physical characteristics 23
Picabo **141**
Plants 50
Playtime 94
Poisons 50-52, 59, 64, 65
Positive reinforcement 54, 87, 90, 92, 99
Praise 77, 87, 97, 99
Preventive care 101, 105, 106
Proglottid **125**
Prolapse of gland (eye) **133**, 134
Proportion 25
Prostate problems 110
Pulling on leash 97
Punishment 60, 87-88
Puppy
—common problems 58
—diet 61
—establishing leadership 77
—feeding 61
—first car ride 53
—first night in new home 54
—health 35, 103
—meeting the family 53
—personality 40, 41, 103
—selection 34-41, 101
—show quality 36, 139-140, 143
—socialization 55
—teething 51, 59
—training 56-57, 77, 89
Puppy-proofing the home 50-52, 81, 83-84
Pyruvate dehydrogenase deficiency 27, 112
Rabies 108, 109
Rawhide 47
Raycroft Springsteen **154**
Razzle **21**
Red **21**
Registration 39
Rescue dogs 34
Retinal disease 136, **137**
Return from Shooting 13
Rewards 77, 87, 97, 99
Rhabditis **126**
Ring procedure 148
Roaming 110
Rope toys 48
Roundworm **122**, 123, **126**
Safety 44, 50-52, 59, 81, 83-84, 94-95
—commands 95
—in the car 53, 76, 95
—outdoors 26, 33, 50-52, 95
—with toys 46-48, 84
Sandiam 15
Sandringham Spark **10**
Sarcoptes scabiei **119**
SARD 137
Scent attraction 86
Scabies 119
Sebastian **80**
Senior dog
—diet 64
—health 105
Sex 35
Shellanbarger, Jo 14
Show potential 36, 139-140, 143
Sir Peter **11**
Sit 90
Sit/stay 92
Size 33
Smokerise Country Gentleman **14**
Snoring 18
Socialization 23, 55-57, 89, 103
Soft toys 47
Soundness 21
Spain 11
Spaying 103, 109-111, 148
Specials 146
Specialty shows 13, 14, 15, 143-144
Sporting Dog Breeder of the Year 15
Sporting Group 144
—first Clumber to win 12
Spot bath 70
Squirrel Run kennel 12
Squirrel Run Nibble 12
Standard 142
Stay 92
Stray dog 75
Supervision 58-59, 84
Surgery 110
Sussex Spaniel 15
Table scraps 65
Taenia pisiformis **125**
Tail docking 25
Tapeworm 124, **125**, **126**
Tattooing 76
Teeth 40, 73, 103
Teething 51, 59
Temperament 40, 103
Terryville 15
Tessa **85**
Therapy dog 99
Thirst 66
Thyroid disease 27, 112
Ticks **117-118**
Timing 85, 94, 99
Tone of voice 78, 87, 99
Torey **21**
Toxascaris leonine 122
Toxins 50-52, 59, 64, 65
Toxocara canis **122**
Toys 46-48, 51, 59, 84
Tracking 16, 21, 99, 150, 154
Training 21
—basic principles 77
—commands 58, 81, 90-97
—consistency in 56, 58, 90, 92
—crate 44, 83-87
—importance of timing 85, 94
—potty 80-87
—proper attitude 78
Traveling 44, 53, 76, 95
Treats 53, 63, 77, 87, 99
—weaning off in training 97
Trichuris sp. **124**
Type 139-140
United States 11-16, 29
United States Dog Agility Association 153
Urine marking 110
Uveitis 135
Vaccinations 35, 52, 56, 103, 105, 109
Veterinarian 34, 46, 48, 52, 95, 103, 105-107, 109
Veterinary insurance 107
Vishnu Quijote Del Cipres **139**
Visiting the litter 38, 41
Vitamin A toxicity 65
Wait 95
Walker, Mrs. Helen Whitehouse 150
Water 65, 83
—bowls 43
—increased intake 66
Weight 25
Westminster Kennel Club 11, 14, 15, 141
West Nile virus 121
Wheatley, Francis 13
Whining 54, 60, 84
Whipworm **124**
Wicksford 15
Wild Cherry's King of Hearts **138**
Williana Clumber Spaniel Club 13
Winners Bitch 146
Winners Dog 146
Woodsman 16
Worm control 124
Yard 26, 33, 51, 95
Young, Betty L. 13-14
Zaleski, Richard and Judith 14

My Clumber Spaniel

Dog's Name _____

Date _____ Photographer _____